Montana

MONTANA BY ROAD

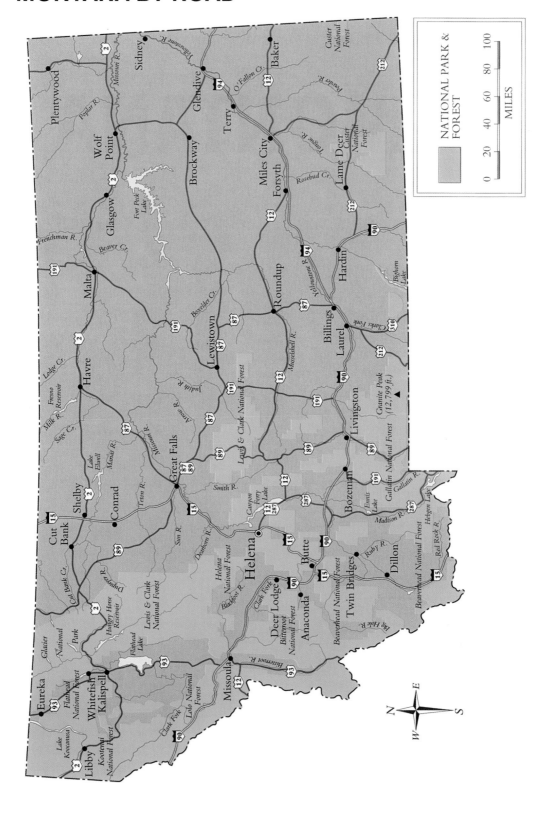

Celebrate the States

Montana

Clayton Bennett and Wendy Mead

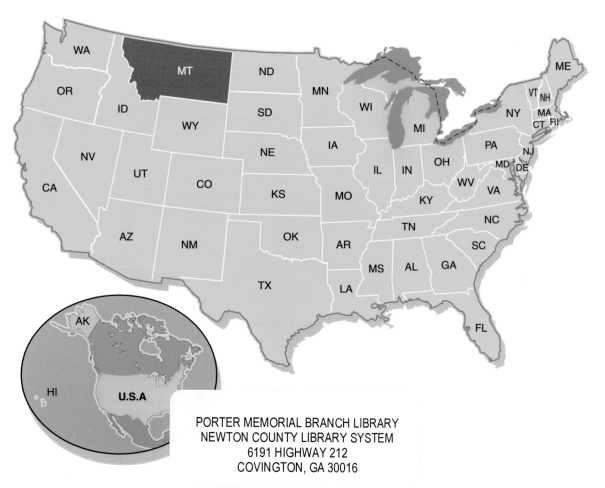

Marshall Cavendish
Benchmark

New York

Other Marshall Cavendish Offices:
Marshall Cavendish Ltd. 5th Floor, 32-38 Saffron Hill, London EC1N 8 FH, UK • Marshall Cavendish International (Asia) Private Limited, 1 New Industrial Road, Singapore 536196 • Marshall Cavendish International (Thailand) Co Ltd. 253 Asoke, 12th Flr, Sukhumvit 21 Road, Klongtoey Nua, Wattana, Bangkok 10110, Thailand • Marshall Cavendish (Malaysia) Sdn Bhd, Times Subang, Lot 46, Subang Hi-Tech Industrial Park, Batu Tiga, 40000 Shah Alam, Selangor Darul Ehsan, Malaysia

Marshall Cavendish is a trademark of Times Publishing Limited

All websites were available and accurate when this book was sent to press.

Library of Congress Cataloging-in-Publication Data

Bennett, Clayton.
Montana / by Clayton Bennett and Wendy Mead.—2nd ed.
p. cm. — (Celebrate the states)
Summary: "Provides comprehensive information on the geography, history, wildlife, governmental structure, economy, cultural diversity, peoples, religion, and landmarks of Montana"—Provided by publisher.
Includes bibliographical references and index.
ISBN 978-0-7614-4731-3
1. Montana—Juvenile literature. I. Mead, Wendy. II. Title.

F731.3.B46 2011
978.6—dc22
2009007939

Editor: Christine Florie
Co-Editor: Denise Pangia
Publisher: Michelle Bisson
Art Director: Anahid Hamparian
Series Designer: Adam Mietlowski

Photo research and layout by Marshall Cavendish International (Asia) Private Limited—
Thomas Khoo, Benson Tan and Gu Jing

Cover photo by Corbis

The photographs in this book are used by permission and through the courtesy of: *Bes Stock/Alamy*: 64, 108, 133; *Corbis*: back cover, 12, 22, 39, 43, 46, 49, 58, 63, 68, 72, 75, 78, 80, 92, 99, 111, 123, 124, 125, 126, 127, 134, 135; *Gettyimages*: 18, 20, 47, 89, 128, 129, 130; *Lonelyplanet Images*: 52; *National Geographic Stock*: 119; *Photographers Direct*: 31, 62; *Photolibrary*: 8, 11, 15, 16, 24, 27, 28, 33, 35, 37, 50, 56, 66, 84, 96, 100, 102, 106, 114, 117, 121; *Photolibrary/Alamy*: 65, 87, 41, 105, 118, 120, 131, 132, 137.

Printed in Malaysia
1 3 5 6 4 2

Contents

Montana is dramatic.

"When you cross the state line heading west from North Dakota, something changes. Suddenly everything looks farther away, even the sky. The state deserves its nickname, Big Sky Country."

—teacher Kent Warren

Everything about it feels big . . .

"The grandest sight I ever beheld."

—explorer Meriwether Lewis, on seeing Great Falls for the first time in 1805

"Montana is big—big in geography, big in history, big in culture and people, all under that beautiful big sky."

—writer Patrick "Paddy" Straub

. . . and beautiful.

"I love everything about Montana. . . . I have spent many days . . . fishing, photographing, and hunting this marvelous big-skied state. I still feel like I'm spending each day in heaven."

—poet and photographer Mike Logan

Montana is part Rocky Mountains . . .

"It is a region of marvelous lakes, towering peaks, vast glaciers, and deep, narrow fiords. . . . [Everyone] comes away filled with enthusiasm for their wild and singular beauty."

—conservationist George Bird Grinnell

. . . and part open prairie.

"It is an empty, lonely place if you are not a wheat farmer."

—novelist Richard Ford

In recent years, many newcomers have settled in Montana.

"I moved here four years ago after coming for a short visit. I love the mountains, snowboarding and the rivers . . . the sunrises on my drive to school."

—a Kalispell schoolteacher

"New faces are everywhere—at the gas station, in the checkout line at the grocery, in our neighborhoods."

—economist Paul F. Polzin

But Montana still casts a spell that's hard to resist.

"Nearly everywhere in this state, even on the fringe of areas thick with development, it is still possible to find, within a short distance, the simple grandeur of the prairie, a quiet meadow, a rippling stream, or a trail leading to a mountaintop where we can drink in the simple freshness that replenishes our souls."

—writer Rick Graetz

More than a century ago Montana became known as the Treasure State because its mountains contained so much gold, silver, and copper. A few people still search for gold. But these days people are just as likely to be digging for dinosaur bones in Montana as precious metals. Still, Montana has many treasures—awe-inspiring landscapes, hardworking people, and a rich history. Come meet Montana.

Chapter One

Tall Peaks, Big Sky

For many the name Montana conjures up images of the Rocky Mountains. That striking feature of its landscape was definitely first in the minds of those naming the area. They chose Montana, which is drawn from the Latin word for "mountainous." The state has much more than just mountains, however. Home to a remarkable range of habitats, Montana has open prairies, lush valleys, and thick forests.

It takes a lot of space to hold that many kinds of land, but Montana is more than big enough. It is the fourth largest of the fifty states. All of New England would fit inside Montana, with room to spare.

THE ROCKY MOUNTAINS

More than 75 million years ago, huge sections of Earth's crust collided in what is today western North America. As they pushed against each other, land was forced upward, forming the Rocky Mountains. Much later, huge sheets of ice called glaciers covered much of the continent. The glaciers scraped out lakes and valleys as they moved, further changing the landscape.

The Bitterroot Mountains, part of the Rocky Mountain Range, straddle Montana's western border with Idaho.

The Rocky Mountains, which extend from Canada to Mexico, include the western two-fifths of Montana. Many different groups of mountains make up the Rockies. Montana has more than fifty of these mountain ranges, including the Anaconda, Bitterroot, Salish, Gallatin, and Flathead. Many of Montana's jagged peaks soar more than 10,000 feet above sea level. Some are covered with snow for ten months a year. At 12,799 feet, Granite Peak in the Beartooth Mountains is the state's highest point.

Up near Canada some of the wildest and most scenic parts of Montana have been set aside as Glacier National Park. Several of the ragged peaks in this park are so sharp and remote that they have never been climbed. The park is also famous for the numerous deep blue lakes that are nestled between the peaks. "I can't believe this place," says an exhausted hiker from Illinois. "We passed the most incredible waterfalls. Saw a mother bear and two cubs up a tree, then saw a mountain goat. I mean it was right there! And then when we got to Iceberg Lake, there were actually icebergs in it! I have to head home tomorrow, but I'm coming back next year."

High up in the Rocky Mountains, many rivers are born as snowmelt tumbles down moss-covered slopes. These trickles eventually turn into cold, fast rivers that are the perfect home for trout. People come from all over the world to fish in the Madison, Gallatin, Yellowstone, and Blackfoot rivers as well as dozens of world-class trout streams.

The nation's longest river, the Missouri, also starts in the Montana Mountains, near Three Forks. It works its way through the state, filling Canyon Ferry Lake and rushing through a gorge known as the Gates of

Lake Saint Mary is just one of the 131 named lakes found in Glacier National Park.

Montana's rivers, including the Madison River shown here, are popular destinations for fly fishing.

the Mountains. After passing through this gorge, the Missouri stretches across the plains, offering many great opportunities for fishing, boating, and wildlife watching at such spots along the way such as Spite Hill and Pelican Point.

THE GREAT PLAINS

Driving east through the Rocky Mountains, you head around jagged peaks and into green valleys, through deep forests and past crystal-clear lakes. Then suddenly the world seems to drop away. Spread out before you are the flat, empty Great Plains. "The landscape of Montana is like what you see on a heart monitor," says Jim Secor, a Lewistown native. "In the west,

LAND AND WATER

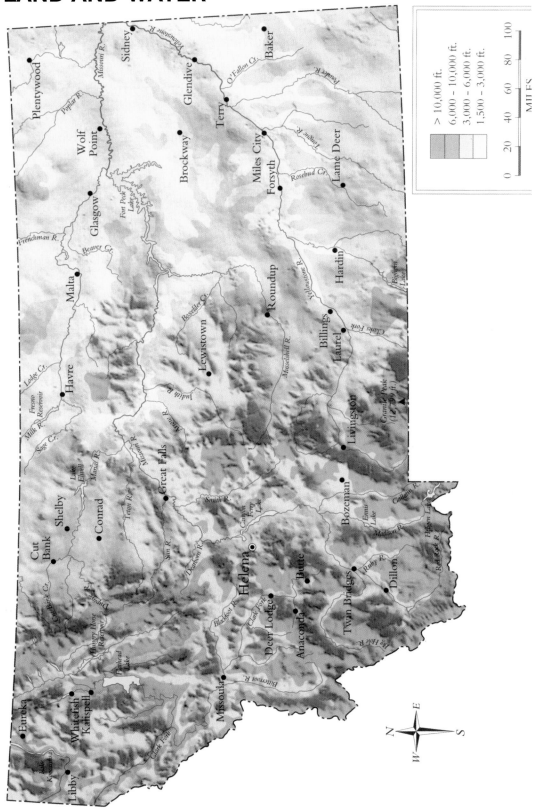

Plentywood

Sidney

Yellowstone R.

Baker

Missouri R.

Poplar R.

Wolf
Point

Brockway

Glendive

Terry

O'Fallon Cr.

Powder R.

Miles City

Forsyth

Lame Deer

Glasgow

Fort Peck
Lake

Rosebud Cr.

Tongue R.

Frenchman R.

Beaver Cr.

Malta

Roundup

Yellowstone R.

Hardin

Bighorn
Lake

Lodge Cr.

Havre

Boxelder Cr.

Lewistown

Musselshell R.

Billings

Laurel

Clark's Fork

Fresno
Reservoir

Milk R.

Sage Cr.

Judith R.

Arrow Cr.

Livingston

Granite Peak
(12,799 ft.)

Lake
Elwell

Maria R.

Missouri R.

Great Falls

Smith R.

Bozeman

Gallatin R.

Shelby

Conrad

Teton R.

Canyon
Ferry
Lake

Ennis
Lake

Madison R.

Hebgen Lake

Cut
Bank

Sun R.

Helena

Butte

Twin Bridges

Ruby R.

Dillon

Red Rock R.

Cut Bank Cr.

Dearborn R.

Blackfoot R.

Clark Fork

Deer Lodge

Anaconda

Big Hole R.

Dupuyer Cr.

Hungry Horse
Reservoir

Flathead
Lake

Eureka

Whitefish
Kalispell

Missoula

Bitterroot R.

Clark Fork

Lake
Koocanusa

Libby

N
E
S
W

> 10,000 ft.
6,000 – 10,000 ft.
3,000 – 6,000 ft.
1,500 – 3,000 ft.

0   20   40   60   80   100
MILES

it has peaks and valleys like a normal heartbeat, and then it goes dead flat." The line where the mountains rise abruptly from the plains is called the Rocky Mountain Front. This area features high cliffs, thick forests, and rich valleys.

The Great Plains cover the eastern three-fifths of Montana. Few trees grow on the rough, dry land. "I used to think you had to have trees where you live," says a man from Billings. "But pretty soon you start seeing sunrises, sunsets, and incredible skyscapes." Indeed, without trees or mountains getting in the way, it seems as if 90 percent of the world is sky. This part of Montana gives the state its nickname, Big Sky Country.

But eastern Montana is not all flat. The Bears Paw, Big Snowy, and Little Rocky mountains rise up from the middle of the plains. An area called the Missouri Breaks in the northeast is filled with broken cliffs and ravines. And in the southeast, wind and rain have sculpted the soft earth into amazing pillars and buttes.

WILD THINGS

While the peaks of the Rocky Mountains are indeed rocky, many of the lower slopes are covered with dark green forests of fir, pine, and spruce trees. Cedar, birch, and ash trees are also common. Juniper and cactus survive in some parts of the arid east. Wildflowers such as lupine, heather, and phlox brighten the mountains. Many Montanans say that nothing is more beautiful than a field of bear grass blooming on a mountain slope.

The mountains are home to a huge variety of wildlife, including moose, elk, deer, black bears, grizzly bears, and mountain lions.

Hundreds of bear grass blossoms blanket a hillside in Glacier National Park.

Glacier National Park is particularly famous for the bighorn sheep and mountain goats that visitors often see darting across its rocky slopes. Montana's grasslands are home to pronghorn antelope, mule deer, and prairie dogs.

Apart from the trout that lure fishers from near and far, grayling, pike, sturgeon, whitefish, and perch also populate Montana's plentiful rivers and lakes. Hundreds of species of birds make their home in Montana, from tiny wrens to huge trumpeter swans. All across the

The least tern nests on sparsely vegetated sand-pebble beaches and islands of large reservoirs and rivers in northeastern and southeastern Montana.

state, eagles and hawks soar, keeping an eye out for prey. Many ducks, cranes, egrets, and herons make their homes near lakes, while owls, woodpeckers, and bluebirds flit in the forests.

Montana is also home to several endangered and threatened species. In the eastern part of the state the least tern has been struggling for survival because of threats to its breeding grounds. It is small in length, ranging from 8.3 to 9.4 inches on average, with an impressive average wingspan of 20 inches. With a distinctive black stripe on its head, white chest, and gray wings, the least tern is easy to spot. This bird likes to nest on sandbars of the Yellowstone and Missouri rivers. Unfortunately, these areas are also popular with people who come to enjoy outdoor activities. Conservationists are working on ways to protect the least tern's nesting habitats.

AN AQUATIC RARITY

Found in the waters of the Missouri and Yellowstone rivers, the pallid sturgeon is facing extinction. This rare freshwater fish can weigh more than 75 pounds and reach more than 6 feet in length. Its life span is equally impressive—the pallid sturgeon can live to be fifty years or older.

The pallid sturgeon's population has been negatively affected by changes in its natural habitats. The construction of dams, dikes, and channels on the rivers decreased the water's turbidity, or muddiness, a condition the pallid sturgeon needs to thrive. The mammoth-size fish was added to the federal list of endangered animals in 1990.

Efforts to revive the species began in the mid–1990s through the use of fish hatcheries. Biologists bring wild pallid sturgeon to hatcheries, where they spawn and then are released. The resulting fertilized eggs stay at the hatchery until the young fish are large enough to survive in the wild. This program is run by the national Pallid Sturgeon Recovery Team.

In 2008 the team saw signs of progress. They had been stocking the Missouri River with hatchery-raised pallid sturgeon since 1998—adding about 4,500 fish above Fort Peck Dam and roughly the same number of fish below the dam. "Our biologists are starting to pick up some of those stocked fish," says Steve Krentz, a biologist with the U.S. Fish and Wildlife Service who heads up the national Pallid Sturgeon Recovery Team. This discovery means that the stocked fish are surviving after being placed in the river.

While not endangered, the American bison (sometimes called buffalo) remains a species of concern in Montana. Thousands upon thousands of these mighty animals used to roam the state until the late nineteenth century, when they were hunted to near extinction. Located inside the Flathead Indian Reservation, the National Bison Range was established in 1908 to help protect this species. About 350 to 500 bison live at this wildlife refuge.

Bison can be found in even greater numbers in Yellowstone National Park. These animals have become the source of controversy because they can carry a disease called brucellosis. Bison are migratory animals and can pass this disease to cattle when they leave the park's boundaries. In the past, bison that roamed away from Yellowstone were sometimes killed to stop brucellosis from spreading.

Once near extinction, the state's trumpeter swan population has grown substantially since the 1930s.

Trumpeter swans are another Montana success story. With a wingspan of up to 8 feet, the trumpeter swan is the largest waterfowl in North America. These majestic white birds used to live all over Canada and as far south in the United States as Missouri. But hunting and human activities took a harsh toll. By 1932 fewer than a hundred trumpeter swans remained in the world. Most were in Montana's southwestern corner.

In 1935 the Red Rock Lakes National Wildlife Refuge was established to give the swans some peace and quiet. Over the years this remote corner of Montana has given the trumpeter population a chance to rebound. Today more than five hundred nest at Red Rock Lakes, and two thousand others arrive each winter from Canada.

DRY TIMES

In addition to wildlife issues the state must also grapple with natural resource challenges. Perhaps the most critical is its water supply. The state receives 15 inches of precipitation per year on average. When it receives below-average precipitation, Montana can experience some challenges. There needs to be enough water available to support agriculture, business, and tourism as well as the daily lives of Montanans.

The state relies heavily on the snow that falls in its mountain areas. In the spring the mountain snowpack melts. The resulting water fills Montana's rivers and streams and collects in its reservoirs. A less-than-adequate amount of snow can cause rivers and streams to become shallower than normal or even to dry out. This means that there is less water for farmers and ranchers to raise their crops or care for the livestock. Tourists who flock to Montana's waterways to enjoy the state's

During the years of drought, once flowing streams, such as this one in the Missouri Breaks, turned into dried-up paths of cracked earth.

famous fishing spots may also find themselves out of luck during times of drought. Dry times can lead to more wildfires as well, a problem that the state has battled many times in its history.

The state experienced drought conditions for seven consecutive years, from 1999 to 2006. Governor Brian Schweitzer described this period as "the longest and most severe episode of drought for Montana since the 1930s." Even in 2008, when experts were predicting a low or moderate impact from droughts, the state still sought federal assistance. The state asked the federal government to declare several counties, including Roosevelt, Dawson, Broadwater, and McCone, as natural-disaster areas because of the effects of below-average precipitation.

A CHANGING CLIMATE

In addition to cycles of drought, the state has also seen some environmental changes. Scientists have found that Montana's average temperature is rising. In response to this trend, the state established the Climate Change Advisory Committee (CCAC) in 2005. Montana has already seen some of the impact of temperature change at one of its most famous sites, Glacier National Park. "One hundred years ago, 150 glaciers glittered along its mountaintops. Only 27 remain today and they all may be gone by the year 2022, should current weather patterns continue," explains Richard Opper, director of the Montana Department of Environmental Quality.

Some areas of Montana have warmed more than the global average of 1.4 degrees Fahrenheit. In Bozeman the average temperature has increased by 1.95 °F over the past fifty years. The state's climate during the month of March has seen an even more dramatic change: Billings

Some experts believe that all of the glaciers in Glacier National Park will disappear by 2022 because of climate change.

has become 6.18 degrees warmer on average, and Bozeman has seen an average increase of 7.7 degrees.

Scientists believe that the rising average temperature is linked to an increase of certain gases in the atmosphere. One of these so-called greenhouse gases is carbon dioxide. While it is normally found in nature, levels of carbon dioxide have risen because of the increased use of fossil fuels, such as coal, oil, and gasoline. These fuels release carbon dioxide into the atmosphere when they are burned to produce energy.

In 2007 the CCAC released the Montana Climate Change Action Plan. The plan called for programs to improve business and home energy efficiency and to encourage the use of renewable energy sources, such as solar and wind power. It made several recommendations regarding transportation, including new standards for vehicles and a fuel-efficient replacement tire program. Dedicated to an environmentally sound future, the state has plans to get 15 percent of its energy from renewable sources by 2015.

Chapter Two

Past and Present

The lands of Montana are rich with history. Paleontologists have uncovered some of its ancient past in the form of dinosaur fossils, which date back millions of years. Dinosaur eggs at the H. Earl Clack Museum in Havre, for instance, are 75 million years old. At the Carter County Museum in Ekalaka visitors can see the full skeleton of a hadrosaur, a duck-billed creature that roamed the marshlands of eastern Montana around the same time.

Human activity in the region is much more recent. Scientists believe that people first came to what is today Montana about 10,000 to 12,000 years ago. The area looked much different than it does today. For instance, about 12,000 years ago, much of western Montana was 2,000 feet underwater in what is now called Glacial Lake Missoula. The state has taken its present shape after centuries upon centuries of environmental changes.

Abundant wildlife and open lands drew the early settlers to Montana.

Known as Paleo-Indians, the area's early inhabitants were hunters and gatherers who lived in small family groups. They were nomads, traveling from place to place in search of food. Traces of this ancient culture have been found in several areas, including the MacHaffie Archaeological Site in Montana City and the Anzick Site near Livingston.

Over time the weapons used by these early peoples evolved. These weapons define different time periods. Archaeologists note that early Paleo-Indians hunted large animals, such as the woolly mammoth, using spears. Around 6000 BCE, they started using the atlatl, a weapon used to launch a dart at a target. These darts were more accurate and worked from a greater distance than did hand-thrown spears. By 500 CE the bow and arrow had become the preferred hunting tools.

One hunting method, however, did not involve tools. Instead it relied on landforms and human ingenuity. A group of hunters would chase a herd of bison and guide them toward a cliff—called a buffalo jump or bison kill. There are about three hundred such sites in Montana, including First Peoples Buffalo Jump State Park in Ulm. After the animals fell over the cliff, they were butchered. Every piece had an important use. The hide was made into clothing and shelters, the meat was cooked or dried for later use, the bones were carved into tools, and the fat was saved for cooking. Even the bisons' droppings were used—as fuel for cooking fires.

Another important animal was the dog. Late prehistoric Indians employed these animals in their daily lives, relying on them to help carry their belongings as they roamed the land. A dog would pull a

The First Peoples Buffalo Jump in Ulm allowed American Indians to stampede herds of bison over a high cliff in order to secure the necessities of food, clothing, and shelter.

travois—a sled made of two poles tied together, with a net or a platform in between them. Around 1750 CE horses were introduced to the native peoples of Montana, who used them for transportation. Guns were also acquired through trading around this time.

LATER NATIVE PEOPLES

By the 1700s many different American-Indian tribes were living in Montana. The Salish (or Flathead), Pend d'Oreille (also called Kalispel), and Kootenai had lived in the region for a long time. The Salish and Pend d'Oreille tribes of the Rocky Mountain region fished, caught small animals, and gathered roots and berries. The Kootenai followed a similar lifestyle, but some took up bison hunting after they obtained horses.

Other groups from the Great Plains moved into the area over time. The Blackfeet are believed to have originally lived in the Great Lakes region but moved into present-day Montana in the 1700s. Around the same time the Assiniboine came to the region from the Lake Winnipeg area.

Horses became a popular means of transportation for Montana's American Indians in the 1700s. They often used a travois, or a type of sled, to haul their belongings.

A CROW LEGEND

Coyote appears in many American-Indian stories. In this Crow legend he creates the world.

In the beginning, before there was anything else, Old Man Coyote stood alone, surrounded by water. Two ducks swam near him, and Coyote asked if they had seen anyone else. The ducks said no, but they thought something might be under the water.

Coyote asked them to go under the water and tell him what they saw. They found nothing, so he asked them to go back. The ducks returned with some roots the second time, and with some mud the third time. Coyote told the ducks to build with the mud, and he made an island out of it. He blew on the island to make it grow. It grew and grew until it became the earth. The ducks thought it was too empty, so Coyote made grass and trees out of the roots.

Coyote and the ducks gave the earth lakes, rivers, mountains, and valleys. But still they were not satisfied. So Coyote took more of the mud and created men and women, and more ducks.

One day, Old Man Coyote was traveling and met another, younger coyote. The young coyote wanted Old Man Coyote to make more animals than just ducks and humans. The older coyote agreed. He created other animals without even using mud. He spoke the names of new animals—"Elk! Bear!"—and they appeared as he spoke. This is how all animals were created.

The Crow also originated from the lands not far from Lake Winnipeg and eventually settled in the southwestern Montana region in the 1800s. The Northern Cheyenne moved into the Powder River area around the same time. By the late 1800s the Gros Ventre homeland stretched from north-central Montana northward into what is now Saskatchewan. Most of these peoples were nomadic, relying on found plants and hunted animals, such as the bison, for their survival.

Other tribes, such as the Cree, Chippewa (also called Ojibwe), Nez Perce, Shoshone, and Sioux, traveled into and out of the region, hunting bison and other game. Before the arrival of the Europeans, the tribes of Montana traded with one another for materials and goods, such as flint, copper, and ochre, a type of pigment. They had conflicts with one another as well. As the eastern part of the United States was settled, many native peoples were pushed westward, leading to more clashes over territory. The introduction of guns in the early 1700s provided some groups with new power. For example, the once-dominant Shoshone were forced out of the area by the better-armed Blackfeet.

CHANGING HANDS

From the late 1600s to the early 1800s the American Indians of Montana were living in lands claimed by France. France was one of the most powerful countries in the world during this time. French explorers who ventured across North America considered the land theirs for the taking. France claimed much of the continent in 1682. That claim, which they called the Louisiana Territory, stretched from the Mississippi River to the Rocky Mountains and included much of modern-day Montana.

Life in what is now Montana did not change much after France claimed it. Few Europeans even entered the area during the next hundred years. The Indians continued to hunt bison and fish as they always had. But farther east, dramatic changes were occurring. In 1776 the American colonies along the Atlantic coast declared their independence from England. They eventually won their freedom after the Revolutionary War. A new nation was born.

In 1803 the United States purchased the vast Louisiana Territory from France. President Thomas Jefferson quickly organized a team to explore the newly acquired land. The group, called the Corps of Discovery, was led by Meriwether Lewis and William Clark. The expedition left St. Louis, Missouri, in 1804, and traveled up the Missouri River in hopes of finding a water route to the Pacific Ocean.

Explorers Meriwether Lewis and William Clark followed the Missouri River until it reached its source in Montana.

By the time the Corps reached what is now Montana, the members realized that the Missouri River would not lead them to the ocean. Instead, they discovered that the mighty river starts in present-day Montana, where three small rivers come together. At this point the explorers could no longer travel by water. They traded their canoes to some Indians for horses and continued west, across the Rockies and on to the Pacific.

On their return east, in 1806, Lewis and Clark passed through the Montana area again. This time the team split up. Lewis led one group north, along the Marias River, and Clark led the other group south, along the Yellowstone River. During their travel east, Lewis and his party encountered eight Blackfeet warriors in July. The two groups decided to camp together, but their pleasant encounter soon turned sour. Lewis told the warriors about the plans the United States had for supplying guns to other groups of Plains Indians. This was a direct threat to the Blackfeet's position in the region, since that tribe had dominated the gun trade for many years. The Blackfeet had been getting their weapons from the Hudson Bay Company, a Canadian fur-trading business.

The Blackfeet decided to steal guns from Lewis and his group, but they were caught in the act, and a fight ensued. Two warriors were killed in the conflict—one by Lewis and the other by expedition member Reuben Field. The surviving Blackfeet fled, and the tribe had a hostile relationship with the United States for years to come because of the bloodshed.

Lewis and Clark joined together again at the Missouri River and traveled from there back to St. Louis. By the end of their travels they had explored more of the Montana area than any other white men.

Lewis and Clark brought back reports of rich lands filled with wildlife. Montana, they said, "is richer in beaver and otter than any country on earth." This caught the attention of fur trappers, who could sell the furs in Europe, where beaver hats were all the rage.

Trading posts were built along rivers. At the posts American Indians and trappers known as mountain men exchanged the pelts for the supplies they needed to live in the wilderness. The demand for beaver pelts was so great that by 1850, trappers had killed nearly all the beavers in North America.

Fur trappers were some of the first Europeans to discover the natural wonders of Montana.

Although the beaver trade dwindled, trading posts continued to operate. They served people who came to the region to hunt bison, establish cattle ranches, and mine gold and silver. Fort Benton, built on the Missouri River in 1846, became a destination for newcomers who hoped to make their fortunes in the territory.

TREASURE IN THE GROUND

After gold was discovered in California in 1849, thousands of people moved to the West Coast hoping to strike it rich. Others looked for gold and silver in Colorado, Nevada, Montana, and Alaska. Most of them did not find gold, but that did not keep them from trying.

Some American Indians in Montana knew where to find gold. But since they did not use it for money, they had no reason to dig it up. A trapper named François Finlay is said to have discovered gold in 1850 at a place called Gold Creek, east of Missoula. Apparently, he kept it a secret. He didn't want to ruin the area for fur trapping.

In 1858 James and Granville Stuart also found traces of gold at Gold Creek. This encouraged others to keep searching. A few years later, in 1862, large gold deposits were found at Grasshopper Creek in southwestern Montana. News of the discovery spread quickly, and fortune seekers raced to Montana.

Almost overnight, the mining camp at Grasshopper Creek became the city of Bannack. Other mining camps sprouted at each new place gold was discovered. Some of these towns disappeared when the gold ran out. Others have endured. For example, Last Chance Gulch is now Helena, Montana's capital.

After the discovery of gold in the 1860s, mining quickly developed into one of the state's top businesses.

With millions of dollars' worth of gold being unearthed in Montana, outlaws soon arrived. They robbed and killed miners and traders. Some towns had sheriffs, but often the law officers were of little help. One of the deadliest gangs, the Innocents, was led by Henry Plummer, also a sheriff for a time. The Innocents killed more than one hundred people before a group of citizens took the law into their own hands. They caught Plummer in 1864 and hanged him at Bannack.

Montana's wildness caught the attention of lawmakers back east. To bring the area under control, the U.S. Congress declared Montana a territory in 1864. Federal law enforcement officers came to the territory, and courts were established to try criminals. As order was brought to the area, more merchants and craftspeople decided to take a chance on moving west, hoping to sell their wares in the mining camps. The camps were becoming cities; the territory would soon become a state.

TOWARD STATEHOOD

As mining towns grew, other settlers followed and built houses, ranches, and farms. Soon settlers were arriving by the thousands. Conflict with the American Indians who already lived there was inevitable.

The U.S. government had signed treaties with American-Indian tribes, promising to keep settlers out of certain areas, preserving them for the Indians. But as more people wanted to move west, the government took land from the Indians and opened it up to white settlers, forcing the Indians onto ever smaller pieces of land.

To make sure the Indians settled in reserved areas, the government cut off supplies and encouraged new settlers to kill as many bison as they could. Without the bison, many Indians starved. Some agreed to move to the new reservations that the U.S. government established for them. Others stayed to defend their homeland.

The U.S. Army was sent out to pacify and settle the Indians who refused to move onto the reservations. But the Indians fought back. One of the most famous battles took place in June 1876, the Battle of Little Bighorn. Thousands of Lakota Sioux and Cheyenne were camped along the Little Bighorn River in southeastern Montana. In command of approximately 650 soldiers, Lieutenant Colonel George Armstrong

Badly outnumbered, the U.S. Army was defeated by American-Indian forces at the Battle of Little Bighorn.

Custer developed a plan to battle this group of Indians. On June 25 Custer divided his forces in three groups, and he led about 210 soldiers to attack the Indian camp from the north. He and all of his men were killed in a conflict that lasted about an hour. The remaining units fought the Indians the following day. Ever since this event, people have debated why Custer attacked the camp when he was so clearly outnumbered.

While the Indians won the battle, they lost the war. Custer's humiliating defeat caused the U.S. Army to step up its campaign against the Indians. Within a decade most Indians had been forced onto reservations.

Montana saw many rapid changes in the 1870s and 1880s. The mining industry grew to include silver, copper, and coal. More and more settlers arrived, building railroads and towns. Ranchers brought herds of beef cattle to graze on the grasslands of eastern Montana. The Wild West was being tamed. On November 8, 1889, Montana became the forty-first state.

MORE THAN GOLD

Most prospectors who came to Montana hoped to find gold, but one found something better. In the 1880s Marcus Daly saw that the demand for copper was growing quickly. Miles of copper electrical lines and telephone lines were being installed in big cities on the East Coast. In 1881 Daly turned a silver mine near Butte into a copper mine. By 1890 he was selling $17 million worth of copper each year. Daly was suddenly one of the richest men in the country. Another man, William A. Clark, was also mining huge amounts of copper in Butte. The competition between them became known as the "war of the copper kings."

The mines in Butte were famous for the amount of copper they produced.

Daly and Clark vied to become the most powerful men in Montana. Daly wanted to have the state capitol built in Anaconda, where his mines were based. Clark fought to build the capitol in Helena, where Daly was not as powerful. Clark also ran for the U.S. Senate. The two men spent millions of dollars trying to bribe lawmakers, and in many cases they succeeded.

Clark won the battle over the location of the new capitol. It was built in Helena, which has been the capital city ever since. But Daly remained rich and powerful until his death in 1900. Though that ended the war of the copper kings, their two companies remained fierce competitors.

CUSTER'S LAST CHARGE

In 1876 George Armstrong Custer led 210 soldiers into battle against a much larger Indian force. Custer and all of his men were killed. Today many people think of Custer as arrogant and foolish. But at the time popular songwriters portrayed Custer as a brave hero and the Indians as savages.

A - cross the Big Horn's crys - tal tide, a - gainst the sav - age Sioux, A lit - tle band of sol - diers charged, three— hun - dred boys— in blue. In front rode blond - haired Cus - ter bold, pet of the wild— fron - tier: A he - ro of a hun - dred fights, his— deeds known far and near.

2) "Charge, comrades, charge! There's death ahead, disgrace lurks in our rear!
Drive rowels deep! Come on, come on," came his yells with ringing cheer.
And on the foes those heroes charged—there rose an awful yell.
It seemed as though those soldiers stormed the lowest gates of hell.

3) Three hundred rifles rattled forth, and torn was human form.
The black smoke rose in rolling waves above the leaden storm.
The death groans of the dying braves, their wounded piercing cries,
The hurling of the arrows fleet did cloud the noonday skies.

4) The snorting steeds with shrieks of fright, the firearms' deafening roar;
The war songs of the dying braves who fell to rise no more.
O'er hill and dale the war song waved 'round craggy mountain side,
Along down death's dark valley ran a cruel crimson tide.

5) Our blond-haired chief was everywhere 'mid showers of hurling lead,
The starry banner waved above the dying and the dead.
With bridle rein in firm-set teeth, revolver in each hand,
He hoped with his few gallant boys to quell the great Sioux band.

6) Again they charged, three thousand guns poured forth their last-sent ball.
Three thousand war whoops rent the air—gallant Custer then did fall.
And all around where Custer fell ran pools and streams of gore,
Heaped bodies of both red and white whose last great fight was o'er.

While the copper kings grew rich and powerful, most miners did not. Work in the mines was exhausting and dangerous. Groups of miners formed labor unions in the 1870s to negotiate with mine owners for better pay and safer working conditions. As more miners joined them, these unions became powerful. A mine owner who didn't agree to union terms might lose all his employees to a competitor.

Eventually different factions within the Butte Miners' Union began fighting for control. In 1914 violence erupted. The group's union hall was destroyed by dynamite during the conflict, and martial law was declared to try to quell the fighting. That same year the unions were disbanded.

THE LAND RUSH

In 1862 President Abraham Lincoln signed the Homestead Act to encourage Americans to settle the West. For a ten-dollar filing fee, settlers could lay claim to 160 acres of government land. If they built a house and stayed on the property for at least five years, the land was theirs. The act was amended to increase the number of acres to 320 in 1909. Settlers could also obtain up to 640 acres of land under the Desert Land Act of 1877, which permitted the sale of public desert lands.

Filing a claim was easy enough, and there was plenty of land available in the Montana Territory. The hard part was making a living from it. Despite Montana's natural beauty, it was not well suited for farming or ranching. Settlers soon discovered that even 640 acres was not enough to graze cattle or raise crops.

Few settlers came to the Montana Territory for the first several years after the Homestead Act was passed. Many people thought it was still too dangerous to live that far west. Mining boomtowns were lawless, and Indians still traveled most of the territory's open land. Homesteaders only took interest after the territory became a state.

The greatest land rush in Montana began in 1908. Railroad owner J. J. Hill promoted settlement in Montana, advertising it as a place of rich farmland and great beauty. At one time Hill controlled three railroads: the Great Northern, Northern Pacific, and Burlington lines. These lines crossed Montana on their way from Minnesota to Washington State. If Montana had more settlers, Hill would have had more business for his railroads.

Hill did everything he could to attract new settlers. He ran advertisements all over the eastern United States and in Europe. He hired agricultural experts to support his claims about farming in Montana. And he lowered train fares for anyone moving there. Soon people were pouring in.

A settler sets up his farm in Sun River during the land rush of 1908.

Miners and cowboys who already lived in Montana were not happy to see so many newcomers. As the cowboys saw it, new residents were spoiling the state's untamed land with their crude farms and houses. Artist Charles M. Russell, who at one time was a cowboy, grew furious as he watched the plains plowed into fields and surrounded with fences. During a speech in 1923 he tore up his prepared notes and said, "In my book, a pioneer is a man who turned all the grass upside down,

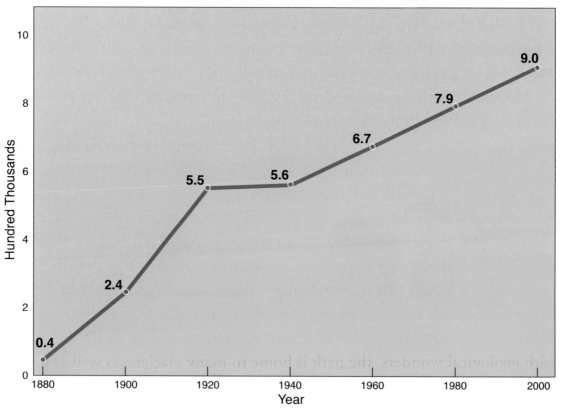

POPULATION GROWTH: 1880–2000

strung bob wire all over the dust that was left, poisoned the water and cut down the trees, killed the Indians who owned the land and called it progress. . . . If I had my way, the land would be like God had made it and none of you would be here at all."

But the settlers believed that farming and ranching would be profitable, and for a while they appeared to be right. Weather was good for several years during the land rush, with high rainfall even in the dry eastern part of the state. Wheat harvests were generous, and it seemed Hill's promises had come true. But drought struck Montana in 1917, and farmers struggled. The following year the rain still hadn't returned. Crops wilted, and the rich topsoil turned to dust. Thousands of farms failed that year, and again in 1919. Banks and other businesses that depended on the settlers and their farms soon closed.

While many left for better prospects, some farmers and ranchers stayed to work the land, and a new wave of settlers came to try their luck. The newcomers learned to work through the dry periods by planting a variety of crops and growing drought-resistant wheat. The number of successful farms grew, and so did the number of land claims. Settlers soon claimed in excess of 80 million acres of government land.

Not all government land was up for grabs by settlers. At the request of President Theodore Roosevelt, Congress set aside some areas of natural beauty to become national parks. One of the first was Glacier National Park in northwestern Montana, which was established in 1910. Filled with geological wonders, the park is home to many glaciers, as well as to lakes, ponds, forests, and wetlands.

The worldwide economic troubles known as the Great Depression hit Montana hard in the 1930s. The state's coal industry ground to a halt as factories shut down and trains stopped running. At the same time Montana was suffering through another drought. Prices for farm goods also fell. Another wave of homesteaders gave up. Whole communities moved at once, leaving their land to be reclaimed by someone else.

There wasn't enough business to keep everyone employed. By 1935, one in four Montanans was receiving help from the federal government. Not all government aid was a handout, however. Some miners and loggers were hired to build roads or put up power lines. Others were put to work building Fort Peck Dam on the Missouri River. When it was completed in 1940, the dam provided water to irrigate crops and generated power for eastern Montana.

Drought and grasshoppers destroyed the corn crop at this farm in Terry, Montana, in 1939.

The Fort Peck Dam was built to help farmers water their crops and to generate power.

The beginning of World War II revived the state's logging, mining, manufacturing, and ranching businesses. The government needed metal for building materials, coal for fuel, and beef to feed the U.S. Army. The country was preparing to go to war, and Montanans were going back to work.

By the 1950s most jobs in Montana were in cities rather than on farms or ranches, so most Montanans were city dwellers. But industry also grew in remote areas. Oil was found in the Williston Basin of eastern Montana, and oil wells soon dotted the landscape.

By this time mining companies were engaged in open-pit mining, in which the earth is scraped away to get to the minerals underneath. Montanans were accustomed to huge mining operations near Butte, so they did not object to open-pit mining there. Then in 1969 mining companies established huge open-pit mines for coal in southeastern Montana.

When people saw the plains torn apart by these mines, they decided it was too high a price to pay for coal. The state legislature passed laws in the 1970s that helped reduce the environmental damage done by open-pit mining. They also raised the mining companies' taxes and used the money to restore the damaged areas.

PROBLEMS AND PROGRESS

Montana has continued to face many challenges in the past few decades. Some of its traditional industries, such as mining, have struggled. In 1980 one of the state's best known businesses, the Anaconda Company, closed its smelter—a metal processing plant—in Anaconda. Once run by copper king Marcus Daly, the company had been bought out by Atlantic Richfield Company (ARCO) in the late 1970s. ARCO shut down the rest of the Anaconda Company's mining operations in Montana in 1983, marking the end of an era.

Montana celebrated its centennial in 1989. Not long after the celebration, the state experienced a political change. It lost a seat in the U.S. House of Representatives because of the results from the 1990 census, which was used to map out the nation's legislative districts. Because of this change, Montana became the second-largest congressional district by area—only Alaska is larger.

By the turn of the century the state was growing in new directions. "Like the rest of America, Montana has transmogrified into a sales-and-service society," says history professor Harry W. Fritz. One area of dynamic growth has been tourism. The number of nonresident visitors increased more than 20 percent from 1997 to 2007. For years people traveled to the state to seek their fortune in its lands; now many come to enjoy its natural wonders.

The state has also been developing its natural resources, from traditional mining to newer forms of energy production. "We're investing in wind farms and we're drilling in the Bakken Formation, one of the most promising oil fields in America," says Governor Brian Schweitzer.

The state, however, was not immune to some of the nation's economic troubles. Fortunately, Montana started off 2009 with a general fund surplus of about $400 million. Weathering the economic downturn meant making difficult decisions about cutting back on spending to keep the state on strong financial ground.

Montana is looking at new ways to create energy, including harnessing the power of wind using wind turbines.

Montana has also had to address security concerns at its border with Canada. As Senator Jon Tester explains, "Because of our rural nature, we have challenges at this border that are different than anywhere else." The U.S. Border Patrol has been building new patrol stations in northern Montana to improve security, and state and federal agencies have been working with their Canadian counterparts to plan ways to manage any problems that may occur at the border.

Over the years Montanans have seen their state through great prosperity and lean times. They have continued to stand strong no matter what the challenge. And they remain optimistic about their future in Big Sky Country.

Chapter Three

Living in Montana

Montanans come from all walks of life—from farmers to professors, from ranchers to business executives. Some are descendants of the American Indians who have lived on these lands for centuries. Others can trace their family tree back to the Europeans who came to Montana seeking a better life.

This rugged and beautiful state has a lot to offer its residents. With easy access to nearly any outdoor activity, it is no wonder that more and more people are choosing to call Montana home. The state's unspoiled beauty and open expanses of land have earned it the nickname the Last Best Place.

EASTERNERS AND WESTERNERS

The landscapes of eastern and western Montana are very different, and so are the people who live in the two regions. They tend to lead different types of lives and have different outlooks.

Easterners are more likely to work on farms or ranches or in the coal or oil business. Billings, Montana's largest city, is in the east.

Many eastern Montanans work on the land as farmers and ranchers.

But generally the eastern part of the state feels more rural, and its people are more conservative. "People here love their God, their families, and their independence," says journalist Becky Bohrer.

Western Montanans are more likely to work in government and education. Helena, the state's capital, is located in the west, as is Missoula, home to the University of Montana. Most of the state's popular attractions, such as Glacier National Park, can be found here, too. Tourists flock to Montana's mountains, and so do most people who move to the state from other places. As a result, western Montanans are more used to outsiders.

People flocked to Missoula's Caras Park for a special celebration.

POPULATION DENSITY

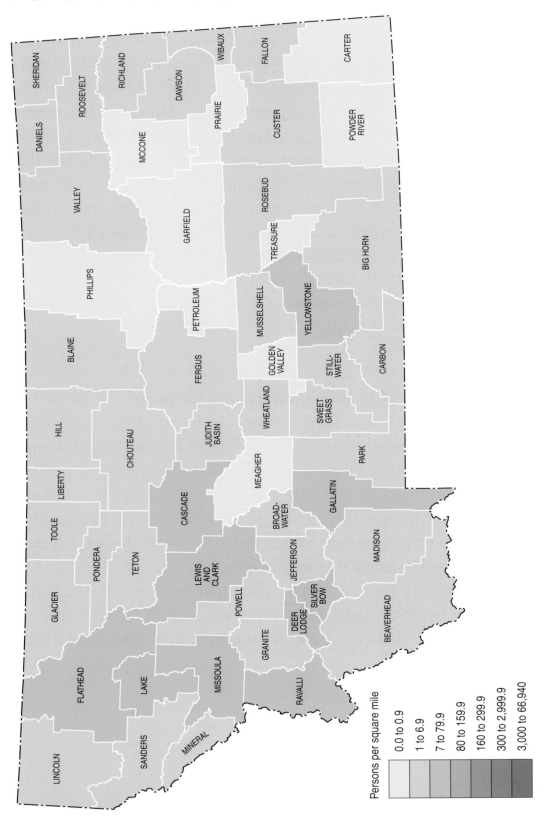

SHERIDAN
ROOSEVELT
RICHLAND
DAWSON
WIBAUX
FALLON
CARTER
DANIELS
MCCONE
PRAIRIE
CUSTER
POWDER RIVER
VALLEY
GARFIELD
ROSEBUD
TREASURE
BIG HORN
PHILLIPS
PETROLEUM
MUSSELSHELL
YELLOWSTONE
BLAINE
FERGUS
GOLDEN VALLEY
STILL-WATER
CARBON
HILL
CHOUTEAU
JUDITH BASIN
WHEATLAND
SWEET GRASS
LIBERTY
MEAGHER
PARK
TOOLE
CASCADE
BROAD-WATER
GALLATIN
PONDERA
TETON
LEWIS AND CLARK
JEFFERSON
MADISON
GLACIER
POWELL
SILVER BOW
DEER LODGE
BEAVERHEAD
FLATHEAD
LAKE
MISSOULA
GRANITE
RAVALLI
LINCOLN
SANDERS
MINERAL

Persons per square mile

0.0 to 0.9
1 to 6.9
7 to 79.9
80 to 159.9
160 to 299.9
300 to 2,999.9
3,000 to 66,940

The state's population is shifting, however, toward the western part of the state. Flathead, Missoula, Ravalli, Jefferson, and Gallatin counties have seen their communities expand by more than 10 percent between 2000 and 2008, according to a report from the Montana Department of Commerce's Census and Economic Information Center. Gallatin County had the largest increase, growing by 32.4 percent during that time period. That same report showed big population declines in many of the eastern counties. This was especially true in Liberty and Treasure counties, which dropped by 20.1 and 26 percent, respectively. Some experts suggest that younger Montanans are moving west to look for better economic opportunities offered by the larger cities there. The west also attracts people from other states because of its breathtaking beauty and low cost of living.

COMMON GROUND

One thing is true of longtime Montanans, no matter which part of the state they call home: they're tough. Living in this beautiful but unforgiving land takes resourcefulness. If the nearest auto repair shop is 100 miles away, people learn how to fix a car themselves pretty quickly. Montanans also learn to take care of themselves at an early age. Rural kids sometimes learn to drive when they're just fourteen, because they are needed to help out on the farm. And many Montanans teach their children how to handle a rifle long before that.

Montana's size and vast, empty spaces give some people a feeling of privacy and freedom. As Paul Hundertmark, a grain elevator operator in Billings, says, "If I can't walk out my back door and shoot a gun, I'm in too big a city."

THE RICH, FAMOUS, AND INFAMOUS IN MONTANA

Over the years more and more people have heard about the good life that Montana offers. In the 1980s outsiders started buying large chunks of Montana. Ted Turner, a wealthy businessman and cable television entrepreneur, established a ranch for restoring more bison to the state. Elizabeth Clare Prophet, the leader of a new-age church, built a compound where she and her followers waited for the end of the world. Other property was sold to celebrities such as actor Tom Cruise. Many Montanans were suspicious and resentful of these wealthy newcomers.

Montanans have grown more comfortable with Ted Turner since he first bought property in the state. His bison herds have grown, and he has shown a commitment to the area. Meanwhile, the world did not end when Elizabeth Clare Prophet said it would. Her church lost most of its members, but the group still maintains a ranch in the state. Just as many of Montana's early settlers did, some newcomers have packed up and gone back home.

But many other new Montanans have stayed. Why leave when they have found paradise? Like the old-timers who wouldn't dream of living anywhere else, they're hooked on Montana's amazing landscapes. As poet Greg Keeler says, "Some of us were born here, and some of us came for the trout."

Montanans mostly keep to themselves. They'll help one another, of course, but most of the time they just look after their own families, businesses, and land—and expect everyone else to do the same. They are experienced at being good neighbors while respecting other people's privacy. An elderly resident of Plentywood boasts, "We still watch out for each other. Nobody steps on anybody else's toes. But we watch out for each other."

In Montana's wide-open spaces, towns are few and far between. What towns there are often have tiny populations with only a few businesses. People in small towns think

Children enjoy outdoor pastimes, such as fishing, in the state's rural areas.

nothing of driving 70, 80, even 100 miles—one way—to Billings or Great Falls to go shopping or to a movie. Although some people might find life in these towns boring, small towners often have busy social lives, filled with an endless array of sporting events, fund-raisers, and church meetings. They know the people in their town, and that's enough for them. "This life—isolated and quiet—is one they have chosen and one they want to keep," points out Bohrer.

ETHNIC MONTANA

Most Montanans—nearly 91 percent—are white. During the mining boom and land rush, great numbers of people from Germany, Ireland, Wales, Norway, and Hungary arrived in Montana. Some Montana towns

ETHNIC MONTANA

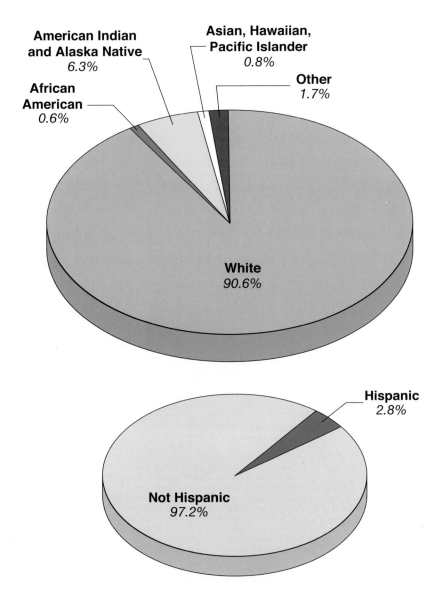

American Indian and Alaska Native
6.3%

Asian, Hawaiian, Pacific Islander
0.8%

African American
0.6%

Other
1.7%

White
90.6%

Hispanic
2.8%

Not Hispanic
97.2%

Note: A person of Cuban, Mexican, Puerto Rican, South or Central American, or other Spanish culture or origin, regardless of race, is defined as Hispanic.

still have strong ethnic identities, such as Glasgow with its Scottish roots and Libby with its Norwegian roots.

Butte in particular has strong ethnic ties that date back to its days as a center of copper mining. The city's Irish heritage becomes apparent each March 17, during its rousing Saint Patrick's Day parade. It is one of the nation's largest, although Butte has fewer than 34,000 residents. The Montana Gaelic Cultural Society also holds a special event in Butte during the summer to celebrate Irish music, dance, and culture.

Many people from Cornwall, in the southeastern part of England, also moved to Butte. One of their favorite foods was a meat pie called a pasty, which came in handy because it was easy to bring to the mines for lunch. Pasties remain popular in Butte to this day.

A group of Hutterite girls gather for a meal in Sweet Grass, Montana.

Many German immigrants settled on the prairie during the homesteading years. Some were Hutterites, German-speaking people from Russia. They had faced intolerance in Europe because of their religious beliefs. They share all goods and property and refuse to serve in the military. Today, about fifty Hutterite communities, each with a few dozen residents, are spread across central Montana. To this day, Hutterites speak German, wear simple clothes, and do not watch television. They continue to live together, raising crops and livestock and taking care of one another. "The Hutterites will do anything for you. They're not afraid of working. They're good people," explains one local who lives near the Prairie Elk Colony in Wolf Point.

MINORITIES IN MONTANA

African Americans, Asian Americans, and Pacific Islanders combined make up only slightly more than one percent of Montanans. Despite being a small fraction of the state's population, these communities are a vital part of the state's history and culture.

African-American communities flourished in cities such as Butte, Great Falls, and Miles City during the late nineteenth and early twentieth centuries. The state's African-American population grew from 183 people in 1870 to 1,834 people in 1910, according to the Montana Historical Society. They worked in the mines, on the railroads, at the state's military bases, and in their own businesses.

Today, African Americans and other Montanans celebrate the state's diversity on Martin Luther King Day. Events are held throughout the state honoring the late civil rights leader, ranging from African-American film festivals to volunteer projects. In Helena there is an annual diversity fair that teaches Montanans about a number of different cultures.

In the early days of the state most of the Asian population was of Chinese descent. More than 10 percent of Montanans were Chinese in 1870. Alone or in families, they came to Montana from California to try their hands at digging for gold. Many of them also helped build the railroads that later carried Montana's products to market. So many Chinese Americans settled in Butte that it is thought the town was one-third Chinese in the early 1900s.

When economic times turned tough, many white settlers blamed the Chinese for their troubles. Within a few years most Chinese in Montana found their way back to the West Coast. Each year Butte honors its Asian past with what it proudly proclaims to be the world's shortest and loudest Chinese New Year parade. Throughout the year visitors can glimpse the world of the Chinese in Butte at the Mai Wah Museum in the heart of Butte's old Chinatown.

More recently the Hmong people from Laos began moving into the state in the 1970s. They had supported the United States during the Vietnam War. After the war ended, they were forced to flee their homeland. The U.S. government helped groups of Hmong refugees immigrate to Montana and other parts of the country.

About 2.8 percent of Montanans are Hispanic, and many have ties to Mexico. Some of the early arrivals from Mexico worked on ranches in the state. Others came in the 1920s and settled in eastern Montana, tending to the area's sugar beet crop. Today, Billings has one of the state's largest Hispanic communities. Each August the city throws a two-day fiesta filled with Mexican music, dancing, games, and food.

American Indians are Montana's largest minority group, making up more than 6.3 percent of the population. Members of the Blackfeet, Salish, Kootenai, Pend d'Oreille, Assiniboine, Nakoda, Gros

Ventre, Crow, Northern Cheyenne, Chippewa-Cree, Little Shell Chippewa, and Dakota Sioux tribes all reside in the state. While most American Indians in Montana live on the state's seven reservations, nearly every county in the state has some American-Indian residents.

Creating economic opportunities for themselves is one of the challenges facing Montana's native peoples. Unemployment on many of the reservations ran as high as 14.8 percent, at the Rocky Boy's Reservation, and 13.1 percent, on the Blackfeet Reservation, in 2008, according to data from the Montana Department of Labor and Industry.

American-Indian tribes are working to improve the lives of their people, often with the support of the state. In 2008 the Crow tribe reached an agreement with the Australian-American Energy Company to build a coal-to-liquid fuel plant that will employ hundreds of tribe members. The state funded a telecommunications project on the Northern Cheyenne Reservation and formed a compact with the Fort Belknap Community Council on gambling.

Montana's American Indians value their history. They share it through stories and language, songs and dances, arts and crafts, and games and ceremonies. Through the warmer months Montana's Indians hold gatherings called powwows. A powwow is a combination of cultural holiday, family reunion, and county fair. The largest powwow in Montana is the Crow Fair and Rodeo. The event draws people from all around the United States and Canada. They travel to Crow Agency, which is located nearly 60 miles from Billings, to be part of it. They camp along the banks of the Little Bighorn River, creating the "teepee capital of the world." The days are filled with wild horse races, Indian foods, art shows, traditional music and dancing, re-creations of historic events, and a rodeo. "Powwows give

INDIAN FRY BREAD

A traditional dish called fry bread is served at almost every Indian event and restaurant in Montana. Have an adult help you make this tasty snack.

2 1/2 cups flour
1 1/2 tablespoons baking powder
1 teaspoon salt
1 cup warm milk
1 tablespoon vegetable oil
vegetable oil (for frying)
cinnamon
sugar

Stir together the flour, baking powder, and salt in a large bowl. Combine the milk and the tablespoon of oil in another bowl. Stir the liquid mixture into the dry mixture until a smooth dough forms. Knead the dough into a smooth ball, then cover it and let it sit for ten minutes. Divide it into eight balls. Flatten each ball until it is 8 to 10 inches across.

Now it's time to cook. Pour enough vegetable oil into a frying pan to cover the bottom, and heat the pan over medium-high heat. Place one piece of flattened dough in the frying pan and cook it until it is golden and crisp. This usually takes one to two minutes for each side. Cook the remaining fry breads. Sprinkle with cinnamon and sugar and enjoy.

At the Rocky Boy's Indian Reservation, Chippewa and Cree Indians maintain a strong heritage through the annual powwow, featuring authentic American-Indian dancers.

people support and strength," says one powwow participant. "Whatever they're coming here for, they usually find it."

THE GOOD LIFE

Most Montanans love the outdoors. It's the reason they live here. Hunting and fishing are a basic part of Montana culture. When a Glendive woman included a picture of herself with a dead deer in the back of a pickup with her annual Christmas letter, her relatives on the West Coast found it strange. But to her it was perfectly natural, because in Montana hunting is an everyday and vital part of life.

But there's more to enjoying the Montana outdoors than just looking for dinner. In places such as Missoula it seems as if every car carries a mountain bike or a kayak or skis. "You always want to be ready in case you can get off work a little early," says one woman.

As the fashionable slopes in Colorado and Wyoming get more crowded, more and more people from out of state are discovering Montana ski resorts such as Big Sky and Big Mountain. Cross-country skiing and snowmobiling are also popular among Montanans. The state has 3,700 miles of groomed snowmobile trails. Most scenic highways are closed to cars in the winter because of snow. But snowmobilers can still get through to visit some of the state's natural wonders in their frozen winter glory.

Winter sports fans love to ride on Montana's snowmobile trails, including this one in West Yellowstone.

VALUING EDUCATION

While quality education is a priority for most Montanans, the state has faced many challenges in making it a reality. It ranked forty-fourth in the nation for teacher pay for the 2006–2007 school year, according to a 2007 survey by the American Federation of Teachers.

To help remedy the problem, the state has established special programs, such as the Quality Educator Loan Assistance Program. This program helps qualified teachers pay off their college loan debt. There are also other programs dedicated to improving teacher training and retention. "An investment in our teachers is necessary for our students to be prepared for a global economy," explains Senator Max Baucus.

The state also helps young Montanans achieve their dream of earning a college degree with Governor Schweitzer's Best and

A Billings schoolteacher takes her elementary class outside for some exercise.

Brightest Scholarship. Since 2005 the program has awarded more than 2,200 scholarships to students across the state. "It is education that brings hope—hope of providing for your family, hope of owning a home, hope of starting a business, and hope to realize your many dreams and aspirations. And it is education that provides the opportunity to get there," says Governor Brian Schweitzer.

Even as the state grappled with the national economic downturn, Montana continued to make education a priority. The state worked hard to establish full-time kindergarten programs in schools across Montana. By 2009 about 93 percent of kindergarten students were enrolled in full-time programs, with more schools expected to offer full-time programs in the next few years.

Chapter Four

Making Laws

Before becoming a territory, Montana was known as part of the wild and often lawless West. The gold rush of the early 1860s created numerous mining camps, often without any official to impose law and order. This led some to seek justice on their own, punishing those they thought had committed crimes.

Statehood presented different challenges, with copper kings Marcus Daly and William A. Clark trying to control Montana's political system in the late nineteenth and early twentieth centuries. Both used their wealth to influence the members of the state government as well as state laws.

Despite these hurdles, Montana was a pioneer in giving eligible women the right to vote in 1914. Eligible female Montanans could vote five years before the passing of the Nineteenth Amendment, which granted all eligible women in the nation that same right. Today that pioneering spirit continues, with Montanans taking an active role in politics and making their voices heard about new laws and policy changes.

The Montana State Capitol in Helena is sometimes called the "Temple of Democracy."

MONTANA PIONEER

Before most eligible women in the United States were even allowed to vote, a Montana native became the first woman ever to serve in Congress. A former teacher and social worker, Jeannette Rankin (right) had led the effort in getting women the right to vote in Montana. In 1916 Montana voters elected her to the U.S. House of Representatives.

In Congress, Rankin fought to get all eligible women in the United States the right to vote. She was also a champion of children's rights and of Prohibition to outlaw the sale of alcohol. Within a few years all eligible women in the United States had the right to vote, and Prohibition became law for more than a decade.

Rankin was best known for her opposition to war. She was one of the few members of Congress who voted against the declaration of war on Germany that brought the United States into World War I in 1917. Her decision was not popular with Montanans, and she was not reelected.

But Rankin remained active in politics. She was elected to Congress again in 1940. And again she opposed a declaration of war, this time against Japan for the bombing of Pearl Harbor, in Hawaii. Explaining her vote she said, "As a woman I cannot go to war, and I refuse to send anybody else."

She did not run for reelection. Although she never again held public office, she continued to work for the causes in which she believed until her death in 1973.

Montana's government is modeled after the federal government. Each has three branches: executive, legislative, and judicial.

Executive

The governor is the head of the executive branch. He or she signs bills, which are proposed laws that have been passed by the legislature, to make them into laws. The governor also appoints members of state boards and commissions. Other executive branch offices include lieutenant governor, secretary of state, attorney general, treasurer, auditor, and superintendent of public instruction. All are elected to four-year terms.

Legislative

The legislative branch is made up of two groups: the house of representatives and the senate. The one hundred representatives in the house are elected to two-year terms, while the fifty senators are elected to four-year terms. The legislators vote on bills and approve budgets. After the legislature passes a bill, it goes to the governor for approval. If the governor signs the bill, it becomes law. If he or she vetoes, or rejects, the bill, it still can become law if two-thirds of both the house and the senate again vote to pass it.

Judicial

The state's courts make up the judicial branch of government. The state's highest court, the supreme court, has seven justices. All are elected to eight-year terms. Each of the judges who preside over Montana's twenty-two district courts are elected to six-year terms. Most serious cases are tried in district courts. Less-serious cases are handled by municipal, city,

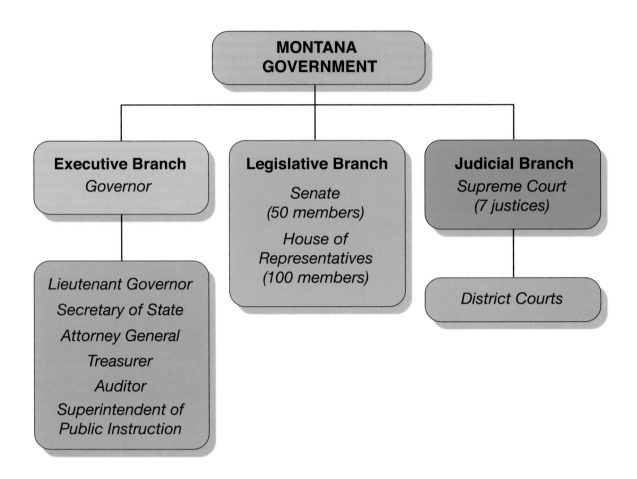

MONTANA GOVERNMENT

Executive Branch
Governor

Lieutenant Governor
Secretary of State
Attorney General
Treasurer
Auditor
Superintendent of Public Instruction

Legislative Branch
Senate (50 members)
House of Representatives (100 members)

Judicial Branch
Supreme Court (7 justices)
District Courts

and justice courts. If someone believes an error was made in a trial, he or she can ask the state supreme court to review the case. The supreme court also rules on whether laws violate the state constitution.

BY THE PEOPLE

In January 1972, one hundred Montanans gathered to create a new constitution. The state's original document dated back to Montana's entry into the Union and had been revised numerous times over the years. Deciding it was time for a fresh start, the members of the 1972 Constitutional Convention came from all walks of life: ranchers, teachers, farmers, lawyers, homemakers, and a few former politicians. The state's supreme court had determined earlier that no current state legislator could serve as a delegate to the convention. These delegates had been selected by their fellow Montanans in November 1971.

The convention strove to have a balance between the two political parties—and also included a few independents—and different points of view. To tackle the tremendous task, the delegates were assigned to different committees to work on procedures or define rights and responsibilities. They met, debated, and crafted the constitution over the course of fifty-six days, with some days lasting until 11 PM.

Their hard work paid off that June, when the state's voters passed the new constitution. Clearly a forward-thinking group, the delegates wrote an article solely dedicated to the environment and natural resources. Section 1 of Article IX reads "the state and each person shall maintain and improve a clean and healthful environment in Montana for present and future generations." They also broke new ground for American-Indian culture. Article X, which covers education and public lands, includes the line: "The state recognizes the distinct and unique cultural heritage of the American Indians and is committed in its educational goals to the preservation of their cultural integrity." Since the constitution was ratified, the state government and the court system have been working on ways to fulfill the promises and duties contained within this legendary document.

The 1972 state constitution stressed the importance of preserving American-Indian culture in its section on education, Article X. The article, however, did not outline how this was supposed to happen or identify the source of funding to support the effort. In 1999 Representative Carol Juneau introduced a bill called the Indian Education for All Act, which was a first step in implementing the goal expressed in the constitution.

The Indian Education for All Act explained that every state resident will "be encouraged to learn about the distinct and unique heritage of American Indians in a culturally responsible manner." It called for the state to include information on each tribe's contributions and history in

A teacher instructs her class on the Blackfeet's native language at a school on the Blackfeet Reservation.

MONTANA BY COUNTY

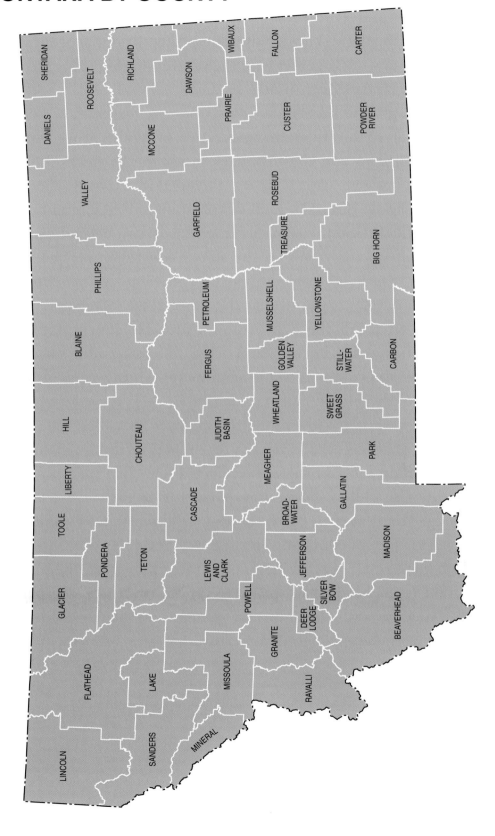

the schools' curriculum. The act also directed educational agencies and state educators to work together with the twelve Montana tribes to create programs to teach American-Indian studies.

Even though the legislature passed the act into law, securing financial support to start the Indian education programs proved difficult. Lawmakers failed to add the necessary funds to the state's 2001 and 2003 biennial budgets. This issue was included in a lawsuit about state funding for schools. Several school districts, including Columbia Falls, banded together to sue the state because its education-funding system did not live up to the terms of the state's constitution. The lawsuit also addressed the state's commitment to American-Indian education. In 2004 a district court found that the state failed to adequately fund the schools and fulfill the constitution's promise concerning Indian education. The supreme court supported that assertion, saying that the state "has shown no commitment in its education goals to the preservation of the Indian cultural identity."

The following year Governor Brian Schweitzer called for a special session of the state legislature to work on education-funding issues. The Indian Education for All program received a one-time special payment of $7 million as well as continuing payments to each district. In the 2007 budget the program received $3.4 million, and $1 million was earmarked for Indian education in the 2009 budget.

Montanans of all ages are beginning to benefit from the program. In addition to creating lesson plans and other materials, the program has sponsored several tribal history projects to gather information for student use. American-Indian culture has also been incorporated

Governor Brian Schweitzer has been working hard to improve Montana's education system.

into mathematics and music classes. Conferences and special training have been offered to educators on how to best implement the Indian Education for All program.

INITIATIVES AND REFERENDUMS

Montanans have the power to influence the laws of their state. They may be asked by the state legislature to vote on a proposed law or constitutional

LEGAL BATTLE OVER SPEED

Montana has a reputation as a place where people don't like the government telling them what to do. The state lived up to its reputation in 1995, when the legislature passed a law doing away with daytime speed limits on the state's largest roads. Instead, the law said people were to drive at "reasonable and prudent" speeds.

A lot of drivers decided the law meant they could drive as fast as they wanted. Cars zooming down the road at more than 100 miles per hour were common. "With no speed limits, it seemed like everything was out of control," says Patti Marnon, a waitress in western Montana. "I've driven into the ditch several times to avoid accidents." Max Johnson of Ravalli agrees. "You can hardly pull out onto the highway," he says. "People can't react at high speeds. It's just nuts."

Many people thought the law just wasn't fair. "What's reasonable to me is not reasonable to you," says one Montanan. Most police officers decided that "reasonable and prudent" meant between 80 and 90 miles per hour. Eventually, the Montana Supreme Court got involved, ruling that "reasonable and prudent" was too vague. When a new law went into effect in 1999 giving the state a top limit of 75 miles per hour, many Montanans breathed a sigh of relief.

amendment. After following a series of steps, state residents can also put an initiative, a referendum (a challenge to a law or act passed by the legislature), or a constitutional amendment on the ballot themselves.

The first step is to send the secretary of state the text of the ballot issue. It is then reviewed by the Legislative Services Division, which may ask for some changes. After the revisions are done, the final text is submitted to the secretary of state and passed along to the state's attorney general to be checked for any legal problems. After receiving approval on the ballot issue, the petitioners can start collecting signatures.

Each type of ballot issue has a different number of required signatures. For an initiative or a referendum, petitioners must get signatures from 5 percent of the state's qualified voters in total as well as 5 percent of voters in thirty-four legislative districts. It is even tougher to put a constitutional amendment on the ballot. Petitioners must gather signatures from 10 percent of the state's qualified voters, including 10 percent in forty districts.

In the 2008 election Montanans were asked to weigh in on several issues, including Initiative No. 155. This initiative called for the creation of the Healthy Montana Kids plan to provide and coordinate health care coverage for children in need. On Election Day Montanans expressed their support for the state's youngest residents by approving the initiative by a wide margin, with 329,289 voting in favor of the measure and 141,701 voting against it. No matter what the issue at hand, state voters are not shy about letting their voices and opinions be heard.

Chapter Five

Montana at Work

In the early days of the state many Montanans made their living from the land. Some raised livestock and crops. Others worked in the mines, harvesting gold, silver, copper, and coal from the earth. Today, most Montanans work in other fields, selling goods and providing services to their neighbors and the state's many visitors.

Still, these early industries remain important parts of the state's economy today. In 2008 there were 29,500 farms covering 60.8 million acres. Wheat is the largest crop, followed by hay and barley. Montanans also grow potatoes, peas, corn, and lentils and tend to a variety of livestock, including approximately 2.6 million heads of cattle.

Mining companies remain active in the state, although not at the same levels as during the industry's heyday. They work to extract silver, gold, copper, and other materials from the state's rich reserves. The Stillwater Mining Company operates two platinum and palladium mines near Nye. Miners at Revett Minerals, Inc.'s two sites—the Troy Mine and the Rock Creek Project—work on removing silver and copper deposits. As has happened many times in the state's history, mining has

Wheat is grown in nearly all the counties in Montana on more than 8,950 wheat farms.

In Gardiner, Montana, just outside of Yellowstone National Park, a miner drills for gold ore.

gone through cycles of boom and bust. The industry lost some jobs in recent years because of the drop in metal prices and in demand for these materials.

Coal production, on the other hand, is expected to flourish. In 2008 plans were announced for a new mine near Roundup at Bull Mountain. This underground mine will tap into the state's extensive coal reserves and will produce about 15 million tons of coal a year. The new Signal Peak mine "will bring a large number of high quality jobs and a strong overall economic impact to the local, regional, and state economy," explains Governor Brian Schweitzer.

Montana already produce a significant amount of coal. In 2008 workers mined more than 44 million short tons of coal. Other businesses employ Montanans to help collect oil and natural gas out of the ground. In 2008, 31.5 million barrels of oil were pumped out of wells in the state. Natural gas is another leading energy product, with more than 6,500 gas wells in operation in 2008. They collectively produced 114 million cubic feet of natural gas.

MONTANA WORKFORCE

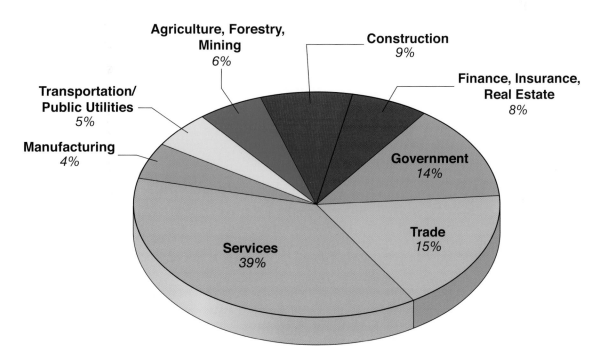

SUPER PIPELINE

In 2008 Governor Brian Schweitzer announced that Montana may get an economic boost from a proposed new oil pipeline that will run through part of the state. Keystone Pipeline, a business partnership between TransCanada Corporation and ConocoPhillips, is seeking to expand its pipeline system from western Canada to the Gulf Coast region in Texas. "The Keystone expansion will be the first direct pipeline to connect a growing and reliable supply of Canadian crude oil with the largest refining market in North America," explains Hal Kvisle, president and chief executive officer of TransCanada.

About 282 miles of the 2,148-mile pipeline will pass through Montana. The state's section will run from Port of Morgan in Phillips County to the South Dakota border in Fallon County. The pipeline will eventually carry up to 590,000 barrels of oil per day.

The cost of this project will reportedly run more than $1 billion just for the Montana section. As it crosses state and county lands, the pipeline will be subject to property taxes. It is expected to raise approximately $60 million in property taxes, with Valley, McCone, and Fallon counties collecting roughly $13 to $14 million each.

PROVIDING SERVICES

Most Montanans work in service-related jobs, such as health care, retail sales, and finance. Out of the state's top twenty employers, eight of the businesses provide medical-related services. Saint Peter's Hospital in Helena, for example, employs more than nine hundred people. Saint Patrick Hospital and Health Sciences Center in Missoula and Kalispell Regional Medical Center are two other large health care providers in the state.

Montanans also work for many national and regional retail chains. Albertsons, which has grocery stores nationwide, is one of the state's leading employers, as is Costco, the popular discount club. First Interstate Bank and Glacier Bancorp Inc. are some of the leading employers in the financial field.

The number of service and sales-related jobs is expected to grow in the coming years, according to a report from the Montana Department of Labor and Industry's Research and Analysis Bureau. As the state's population continues to increase, there will be a greater demand for teachers, nurses, and home health care aides. More business managers, accountants, office clerks, and administrative assistants will also be needed.

VISITORS WELCOME

Roughly 10 million people decided to visit Big Sky Country in 2008, which helped support the state's more than 44,800 workers in travel-related jobs. Montanans provide a variety of goods and services to tourists, from serving food to acting as guides to selling gasoline or souvenirs.

Visitors examine one of the many exhibits at the Museum of the Rockies.

The state's main attractions are Glacier National Park and Yellowstone National Park, each drawing more than 2 million visitors in 2007. But a growing number of tourists are checking out other natural wonders found in the state. Fort Peck Lake experienced a 17.8-percent increase in visitors from 2006 to 2007, according to a report by the Institute for Tourism and Recreation Research. Another site increasing in popularity is the Museum of the Rockies, which saw a 43.1-percent increase in visitors over the same period.

The busiest time for Montana's tourism industry is July through September, with more than 4.6 million out-of-state visitors checking out the state, followed by more than 2.6 million out-of-state visitors

MAKING MOVIES IN MONTANA

With its breathtaking and varied scenery, it is no surprise that Montana is popular with filmmakers. *The Big Trail* (1930) starring John Wayne was just one of the old movies to feature the state. Montana was also the setting for *A River Runs Through It* (1992), starring Brad Pitt and Craig Sheffer, based on the book by Montanan Norman Maclean. It was filmed in part in Livingston and Paradise Valley. Montana also offers many great locales for television shows, documentaries, and commercials. All these types of film projects contribute to the state's economy in many ways, including hiring Montanans to work on the productions and renting out hotel rooms or other accommodations.

The Montana Film Office was established in 1974 to encourage more companies to use the state as the backdrop for their projects. State legislators further enhanced the state's appeal by passing the Big Sky on the Big Screen Act in 2007, which provides special tax breaks for film companies working in Montana. The act calls for companies to receive a 14-percent rebate on local labor costs and a 9-percent rebate on production-related expenses incurred in the state, such as lodging and supplies.

According to the Montana Film Office, eighty-six film and television projects were made in Montana in 2007, bringing in roughly $7.8 million in related spending and creating more than two hundred full-time jobs. One big-screen project, *My Sister's Keeper* (2009), filmed in Montana for only a week. Still, the production was able to make a "direct economic impact of $225,000, which means a total economic impact of $345,000, all in just a few short days," explains Anthony Preite, director of the Montana Department of Commerce.

from April through June, according to 2009 data from the Institute for Tourism and Recreation Research. Most of these visitors come from Washington, California, and neighboring Idaho. The state, however, is working hard to boost year-round tourism, especially during the winter months.

To attract winter sports enthusiasts, the Montana Promotion Division has run special advertising campaigns in certain areas. It also operates a website dedicated to winter activities, such as skiing, snowboarding, and snowmobiling. To continue to develop its tourism industry, Montana has a 4-percent lodging facility use tax, or bed tax.

2007 GROSS STATE PRODUCT: $34 Million

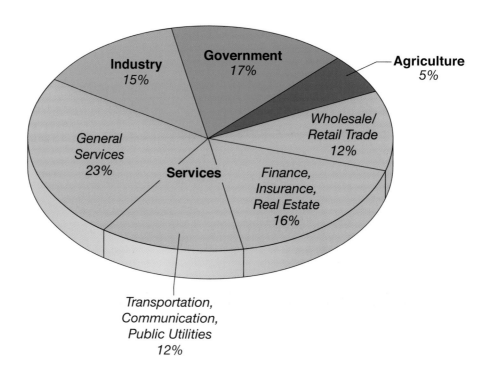

About 70 to 80 percent of wheat grown in Montana is shipped overseas and sold in Asian countries.

Hotels and other facilities collect these funds from their guests, and these monies are used to expand the state's promotional efforts and to enhance its attractions and events.

SELLING MORE GOODS ABROAD

The state experienced significant growth in 2006 in the amount of products it sells to other countries, with an increase of 17.9 percent over the previous year: exports totaled more than $2 billion worth of commodities in 2008. Wheat, Montana's top export, comprised $613.4 million of that total. Chemical shipments also rose by 31 percent that year to reach the $345 million mark. Other major exports included metal ore, vehicles and related parts, mineral fuel, and minerals.

Nearly a third of the state's exports went to its neighbor to the north. Canada bought about $584.7 million of Montana's goods in 2008—a 18-percent increase over the previous year. The state's second-largest trading partner, Japan, accounted for $130.8 million of its total 2008 exports. To support relations with this Asian nation, Montana has a trade office in the Kumamoto Prefecture, or state. There is also another Montana trade office for the Asia Pacific region in Taipei, Taiwan.

State officials and business leaders have traveled the world to expand the markets for Montana's products as well as to attract new businesses. In 2007 a trade delegation visited Japan "to promote Montana and U.S. beef as safe and healthful," explains Joel A. Clairmont, deputy director of the Montana Department of Agriculture. Governor Brian Schweitzer visited Alberta, Canada, around that same time to encourage Canadian companies to consider moving or expanding their operations into Montana.

NAVIGATING UNCERTAIN TIMES

Like many other states, Montana has experienced hardship during the nation's periodic economic downturns. Many parts of the country experienced financial difficulty around 2006, as people began to struggle with paying their home loans. Many mortgage companies, which provided those loans, ran into trouble as more and more of their customers could not make their payments. Some of the mortgage companies went out of business, and the problem eventually spread to some of the banks and investment firms that had bought those mortgages as investments. Several of those companies were either bought by other financial institutions or went bankrupt.

As home construction has slowed, the demand for Montana lumber has decreased.

According to the *Montana Business Quarterly*, Montana fared well during the mortgage crisis compared to other states. As of September 2008, fewer Montanans had difficulty with their mortgages—only 1.5 percent were seriously behind in making payments, or delinquent. This was less than half the nation's average of 3.6 percent. This national crisis, however, did affect the state's real estate and construction industries. The number of existing homes sold declined by 19 percent from June 2007 to June 2008, and the number of new homes being built dropped by 34 percent over the same period.

The state's manufacturing industries were also hit hard. As home construction declined, so did the demand for construction supplies. In 2008, for example, Stimson Lumber Company closed its plywood mill in Bonner. Plum Creek Timber Company cut back its operations in the state and announced the permanent closure of its sawmill in Ksanka. The lumber industry has "been severely impacted by the battered housing market," explains Rick Holley, president and chief executive officer of Plum Creek.

EARNING A LIVING

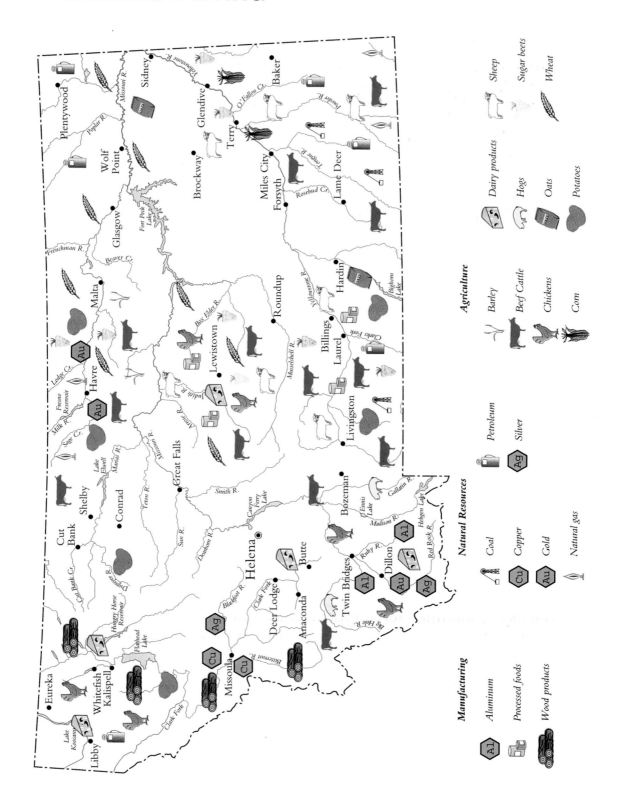

Agriculture

Barley · Beef Cattle · Chickens · Corn · Dairy products · Hogs · Oats · Potatoes · Sheep · Sugar beets · Wheat

Natural Resources

Petroleum · Silver · Coal · Copper · Gold · Natural gas

Manufacturing

Aluminum · Processed foods · Wood products

Even in difficult times Montana found ways to prosper. The state has been successful in developing its energy industry. In 2008 the German wind turbine maker Fuhrlander announced that it was going to build a production and assembly plant near Butte. The plant is expected to employ 150 people, but that number may grow to include an additional 600 positions. For choosing to set up shop in Montana, the company received special incentives as part of the state's clean and green energy development program.

THE YEARS AHEAD

While no one can predict the future, experts remain cautiously optimistic about Montana's economy. The state experienced several years of strong growth and low unemployment prior to 2008. Unemployment in Montana still remains below the national average, at 6.7 percent compared to 9.4 percent in July 2009. "Montana is poised to be competitive in the uncertain economic future of the next few years. Growth in emerging markets has increased demand for Montana's natural resources and agricultural products," explains Senator Max Baucus.

At a time when many companies were scaling back their operations, Montana was attracting new business ventures in a variety of fields. GE Commercial Finance, part of General Electric, opened an office in Billings in 2008. To help establish this new office, the state provided the company with a $1 million workforce-training grant. GE Commercial Finance also received $375,000 to purchase office equipment from the Big Sky Economic Development Trust Fund.

In addition to financial incentives, Montana has a lot to offer businesses, with its low labor costs and educated workforce, not to mention the quality of life employers and employees can enjoy while living and working in the Last Best Place.

Chapter Six

Touring the Treasure State

With its varied terrain, Montana has something for everyone. Hikers can explore 700 miles of trails in Glacier National Park while fishers can see what they can catch in the state's trout-filled streams. Winter snows attract skiers and snowboarders to ski areas such as Blacktail Mountain and Big Sky Resort.

Montana also invites visitors to learn about its history and cultures. Tour a ghost town or retrace the steps of explorers Meriwether Lewis and William Clark. For those interested in American-Indian culture, wander through the Museum of the Plains Indian in Browning or the Sioux Culture Center and Museum in Poplar. Nearly every destination in the state offers visitors a chance to experience Montana's wondrous landscapes, wildlife, culture, and history.

Montana has many great places to ski, including the slopes of the Big Mountain Ski Resort in Flathead Valley.

GOING-TO-THE-SUN ROAD

President William Howard Taft established Glacier National Park in 1910. Previously, the area had been a forest preserve. Sightseeing was challenging in the early days of the park. Visitors had to take a train to the park and then journey by horseback—sometimes for several days—to reach its different hotels and lodges. To attract more visitors, officials decided to build a road across the mountains. The work on this difficult undertaking started in 1921.

Glacier's mountain passes are so steep that some people thought building a road would be impossible. Hundreds of men moved thousands of tons of rock to create the road. The scenery around them was gorgeous but terrifying. One man who worked on the road later recalled, "On several occasions men stood at the top of the cliff, looked down the ladder, and turned in their resignations." The brave men who didn't quit completed the road in 1932. The following year it was officially named the Going-to-the-Sun Road at its dedication ceremony at Logan Pass—the road's highest point, at 6,646 feet in elevation.

Even today the Going-to-the-Sun Road is an adventure to drive. In some places it's nothing more than a ledge carved out of the mountainside. Vehicles longer than 21 feet or wider than 8 feet (including mirrors) are not allowed on the steepest and narrowest sections of the road. There is a height restriction of 10 feet in some places as well. The views are so amazing that many visitors prefer to ride on buses. This way they can watch the breathtaking scenery and let someone who is more familiar with the roads take the wheel.

Any tour of Montana should start with its best-known site, Glacier National Park. The park is famed for its majestic mountains, glowing lakes, and unspoiled beauty. The surroundings are so impressive that you can point a camera in any direction and get a good picture. Glacier National Park is one of Montana's top attractions.

There are only a few roads in the park, but dozens of hiking trails that cover hundreds of miles. These trails offer some of the best chances to see large wildlife anywhere in the country. Wolves, moose,

A hiker takes in the breathtaking view from a trail near Lower Grinnell Lake in Glacier National Park.

and deer are just some of the animals that call the park home. One visitor was getting a good look at a mountain goat when suddenly it took off. "She came out of the trees right at me," he exclaimed. "I had to jump back to avoid being skewered." A surprising number of visitors even see grizzly bears tearing up old logs looking for food. Bears can be dangerous, though, so park rangers advise hikers to clap their hands and shout periodically on the trails so bears know someone is coming and have time to hide or run away. Never surprise a bear!

In contrast to the dramatic sights of Glacier National Park, Flathead Lake to the south seems almost serene. Says one visitor, "Even the Oregonians in our group—who are used to beautiful landscapes—fell into a state of hushed awe."

Roughly 30 miles long and 15 miles wide, Flathead Lake is the largest natural freshwater lake west of the Mississippi River. The lake is famous for fishing and is popular with boaters, swimmers, and water-skiers.

Flathead Lake is a great spot for fishing and boating.

One highlight of Flathead Lake is Wild Horse Island, where a few wild horses can still be found. There are also a lot of bighorn sheep and big birds, including ospreys and bald eagles.

Not far from Flathead Lake you have a chance to see one of Montana's most famous animals—the bison. Once plentiful on the Great Plains, the peaceful herbivores, or plant-eating animals, were nearly wiped out by the early twentieth century. In 1908, 19,000 acres in the Flathead

PLACES TO SEE

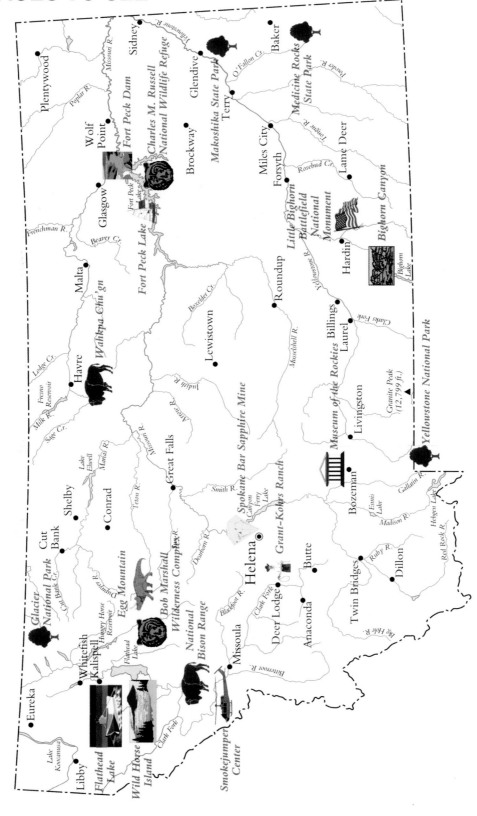

At the National Bison Range, visitors can watch these amazing animals roaming free.

Valley were set aside for the bison to run free. Today the National Bison Range is home to about 350 to 500 of the shaggy animals. You can walk along a nature trail, but people are not allowed on the open range—the bison prefer it that way. While there, you may also see elk, coyote, and ground squirrels as well as more than two hundred species of birds.

Northwestern Montana is also the site of the Bob Marshall Wilderness Complex. "The Bob," as it is known, covers more than 1.5 million acres and includes three wilderness areas: the Great Bear Wilderness, the Bob Marshall Wilderness, and the Scapegoat Wilderness. It is home to elk, deer, grizzly bears, and wolves. Patient visitors may also see bighorn sheep, cougars, lynxes, bobcats, and otters. As a wilderness area rather than a park, the Bob has no recreational facilities. Instead, it offers some of the most beautiful and challenging hiking trails in the state. If you can get by without shelter, electricity, or plumbing, the Bob is an ideal place for camping, climbing, rafting, and snowshoeing.

In 1841 Father Pierre-Jean De Smet, a Jesuit priest, founded Saint Mary's Mission in the Bitterroot Valley, surrounded by gentle mountain peaks. He intended to provide religious teachings to the Salish and Nez Perce Indians in the area at the first attempt at a European settlement in Montana. The mission grounds were sold off in 1850 and then became known as Fort Owen. A new Saint Mary's Mission was established in 1866 by Father Anthony Ravalli, south of the original site in what is now Stevensville. Today the simple church looks very much like it did then. And visitors can still see the same sweeping view of the Bitterroot Mountains that inspired Father De Smet to settle there nearly 170 years ago.

Nestled in the Bitterroot Valley, stands Historic Saint Mary's Mission, which is open to the public.

After all this wild outdoors, you might want to stop in Missoula to get a taste of city life. Missoula is a pleasant, lively city filled with restaurants and beautiful buildings from a hundred years ago. It seems to combine the best of everything—a sophisticated city in the middle of the wilderness.

While you're in town, be sure to visit the Aerial Fire Depot and Smokejumper Center, the nation's largest training center for smokejumpers, the people who parachute into forest fires. The center is filled with videos and exhibits about the dangerous job. You can also take a tour of the training center and the parachute loft. Perhaps you'll even see a plane full of smokejumpers heading out to fight a fire.

The Aerial Fire Depot and Smokejumper Center, the nation's largest training base for smokejumpers, is located in Missoula.

THE SOUTHWEST

In the 1850s a man named Johnny Grant started taking his cattle to the Deer Lodge Valley for the winter. He built his first home there in 1859, and his ranch thrived over the years. In 1862 Grant started construction on the lodge that still stands today. The home is known as the Grant-Kohrs Ranch and is a national historic site. Visitors can tour the elegant ranch house and explore the blacksmith shop, bunkhouse, and other buildings, where park rangers talk about the hard work required of the West's early ranchers. The best time to visit the ranch is during the Grant-Kohrs Days in July. Members of the ranch staff show how to groom horses, round up cattle, brand calves, and harvest hay. There are also blacksmithing demonstrations, wagon rides, and old-time Food cooked on a real chuck wagon.

If you want to find real treasure during your trip around the Treasure State, head to the Spokane Bar Sapphire Mine, next to Hauser Lake near Helena. Amid the bare hills and scrubby juniper bushes, visitors dig through gravel looking for sapphires. Not everyone find them, and the ones they find may not be very big, but people keep trying. "Coming here to dig in the dirt is better than sitting at home," explains a visitor from Washington on vacation in Montana with his family. "If you do find something, it's just real neat. If you don't, it's just fun to get out." The largest sapphire found there weighs 155 carats. People have also found garnets, diamonds, topaz, and rubies.

After searching for your own treasure, you may want to check out Bannack, the site of Montana's first major gold rush. Walking down the ghost town's dusty streets is an eerie experience. At any moment you expect a tumbleweed to roll by or a stagecoach to come roaring around a corner. After gold was discovered there in 1862, the population jumped to more than three thousand in just one year. More than sixty buildings from the gold rush days are still standing, including houses, a hotel, a church, and Montana's first jail. Some people say the hotel is the most photographed spot in Montana. If you want to see Bannack at its liveliest, visit during Bannack Days in July. The festival includes wagon rides, a fake gunfight on the main street, and old-time dancing.

Many miners who left Bannack headed for Helena, where gold had been discovered at Last Chance Gulch in 1864. So many people struck it rich there that by 1888, Helena was home to fifty millionaires. It was the wealthiest city per person in the nation. Much of Helena's past is still visible, from the millionaires' lavish mansions to one-room buildings that housed miners. Explore the community's storied past at the Montana Historical Society Museum or the Original Governor's Mansion. You can also tour the state capitol. Another Helena highlight is the Cathedral

Formerly a copper mine, the Berkeley Pit is now filled with polluted water.

of Saint Helena. This glittering church boasts two 230-foot-tall towers, a white marble altar, and amazing stained glass windows.

Before leaving Montana's old mining region, stop by Butte to see Berkeley Pit. Once the nation's largest open-pit copper mine, it is now a huge mess. It's 1,780 feet deep and 1 mile across, and is filling with water—poisonous water. The pit is a vivid reminder of what people can do to the land.

NORTH-CENTRAL MONTANA

Just east of the jagged Rocky Mountain Front is a dry and windy land of grass-covered hills and plains. Today the area produces a tremendous amount of wheat and barley. But long before humans settled here, it was dinosaur country. Scientists have found entire nests of dinosaur eggs at Egg Mountain, which gave them a lot of clues about the behavior of the ancient creatures. Egg Mountain is the site of the world's first discovery of dinosaur eggs with tiny dinosaurs in them.

You can also glimpse more of the state's history in other parts of north-central Montana. Before American Indians had horses or guns,

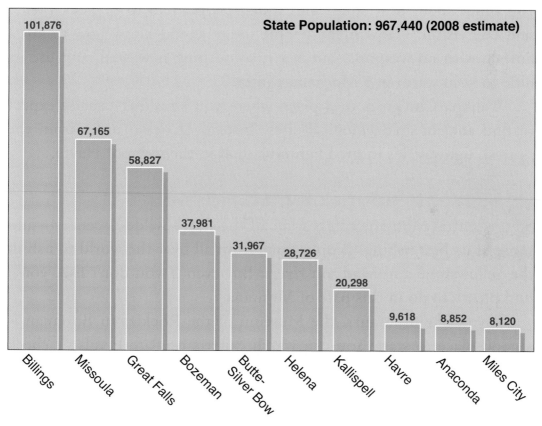

TEN LARGEST CITIES

State Population: 967,440 (2008 estimate)

City	Population
Billings	101,876
Missoula	67,165
Great Falls	58,827
Bozeman	37,981
Butte-Silver Bow	31,967
Helena	28,726
Kallispell	20,298
Havre	9,618
Anaconda	8,852
Miles City	8,120

they used a simple method to kill bison. They would wait until a herd of bison was near a cliff and then startle the animals near the back of the herd. The bison would stampede, and some would be unable to stop running before they reached the cliff. They would fall to their death below.

Cliffs like these are called buffalo jumps or bison kill sites. One of the largest and best-preserved bison kill sites on the Montana plains is Wahkpa Chu'gn. At the site you can see displays of artifacts found there and learn more about how Indians used bison. "It really makes you think about how smart and tough people had to be back then," said one visitor. "How many people today would know how to kill a buffalo with no weapons, butcher it so nothing is wasted, and use its hide to keep warm in a Montana winter?"

Wahkpa Chu'gn is in a place where you wouldn't usually expect to find ancient archaeological sites. Instead of being miles from the nearest highway, it's located behind a mall in the town of Havre.

SOUTH-CENTRAL MONTANA

South-central Montana offers some of the state's wildest scenery—and some of its best fishing. People come from all over the world to fish in the Yellowstone and Madison rivers. But even if you don't fish, you'll find plenty to do in this part of Montana.

If you like dinosaurs, the Museum of the Rockies in Bozeman is a good place to start. You can watch experts prepare fossils or check out an exhibit with an animated *Triceratops* looking for food. At the museum you can also learn about how the Rockies were formed and about the people who have lived there through the centuries.

To see the best of the Rockies, head to Red Lodge. There you can get on Beartooth Highway, which journalist Charles Kuralt called "the most beautiful roadway in America." The road has so many steep climbs and hairpin turns that drivers need three hours to travel less than 70 miles. At its highest point the road reaches an elevation of nearly 11,000 feet. The road is so high that it can snow there anytime—even in July. You never know when you might get into a snowball fight. From the summit you can see for miles. All around you are glaciers, meadows, and mountaintops—including Granite Peak, the tallest mountain in Montana.

Driving Beartooth Highway would be worth it even without the incredible views, because it leads to Yellowstone National Park. The world's

Take a drive on the Beartooth Highway to see some of Montana's most beautiful views.

first national park, Yellowstone contains jagged canyons and dramatic waterfalls. But it is probably most famous for its boiling hot springs and shooting geysers. Most of the park is in Wyoming, but a section of it is in Montana, and three of its five entrances are there.

THE EAST

Eastern Montana is a world apart. The land is dry, flat, and bare. In some places you can travel for miles without seeing a tree or a hill, much less a forest or mountain. Instead, there are just the plains with a sky that never seems to end. This kind of scenery takes some getting used to, but

See the fascinating formations at the Mammoth Hot Springs inside Yellowstone National Park.

once that happens, many people find they can't get it out of their minds.

A dam may not seem like an interesting place to visit, but Fort Peck Dam in the northeast is worth a trip. It stands as a monument to human achievement. The dam is 21,026 feet long and 250.5 feet high at its tallest point. While it was being built in the 1930s, the dam provided work for 50,000 people. The museum at the dam offers a peek at Montana's distant past, with a display of fossils found in the area, including the skull of a *Triceratops*.

Fort Peck Dam backed up the waters of the Missouri River to create Fort Peck Lake, which stretches for 134 miles. The huge expanse of water makes fishers happy, as the lake is full of walleye, sauger, smallmouth bass, lake trout, and northern pike.

THE MOUNTAIN MAN RENDEZVOUS

History comes to life each summer just north of Red Lodge. At the Mountain Man Rendezvous, history lovers get together to re-create the world of the trappers and traders. The event brings back the sights, sounds, smells, and flavors of long ago.

In the 1800s mountain men gathered once a year to sell goods and stock up on supplies for the coming year. The Mountain Man Rendezvous continues that tradition. During the gathering, participants buy and sell goods. Sellers must dress in the clothing of the time. And they can only sell goods that were available then, such as beadwork, dolls, and handmade knives. The event also includes musical performances, reenactments, and demonstrations of old-fashioned skills such as blacksmithing and shooting black-powder rifles.

In the nineteenth century a rendezvous usually included gambling, robberies, fistfights, and shootings. Gunfights break out at today's rendezvous, too, but they are always staged. As the event's organizers say, "Everybody is shooting blanks, and we all have dinner together later on."

Fort Peck Lake is entirely surrounded by the Charles M. Russell National Wildlife Refuge, which protects the most intact section of all the northern plains. This rugged country is no gentle grassland. Instead, it is a maze of bluffs, buttes, and ravines. This is hard land for people to live in, but elk, mule deer, coyotes, bighorn sheep, and countless other animals thrive here.

Unusual geological wonders dot the lands of Medicine Rocks State Park, which is considered sacred ground by some American Indians.

Eastern Montana also has some rough land. At Makoshika State Park, just outside of Glendive, strange pillars and buttes have been formed by wind and water eating away at the land. Farther south, at Medicine Rocks State Park, the wind has carved holes and tunnels in huge rocks standing alone on the grassland. The effect is eerie but beautiful.

Another beautiful spot is Bighorn Canyon National Recreation Area, where cliffs tower above Bighorn Lake. Boaters can't get enough of Bighorn Canyon. The area also attracts wildlife lovers, who come to see peregrine falcons swooping through the sky and Pryor Mountain horses running free.

Let's end our tour of the Treasure State at the site of the most famous event in Montana's history, the Battle of the Little Bighorn. When you visit Little Bighorn Battlefield National Monument today, you might wonder why such a dry, treeless place was so important to the American Indians or the U.S. government. In fact, the site itself was not very important. It was simply one of the places where the two cultures fought for control of the land—and the future.

Looking around from the headstones on Last Stand Hill or the 7th Cavalry Monument, you see nothing but the Little Bighorn River and some grass-covered hills. Most of the year the grass is dry and brown. Only a square around the 7th Cavalry Monument and the visitor center is kept green. "This place keeps two things alive," one visitor commented. "The lawn and our memories."

THE FLAG: *The Montana flag displays the name of the state in large gold letters against a blue background. Below the name is the state seal. The flag was adopted in 1905.*

THE SEAL: *The state seal, adopted in 1893, shows mountains and the Great Falls of the Missouri River as symbols of Montana's scenery. Below them are a plow, shovel, and pick, which represent farming and mining. The state motto appears at the base of the seal.*

State Survey

Statehood: November 8, 1889

Origin of Name: *Montana* comes from a Latin word meaning "mountainous"

Nicknames: Big Sky Country, Treasure State, Last Best Place

Capital: Helena

Motto: *Oro y Plata* (Gold and Silver)

Animal: Grizzly bear

Bird: Western meadowlark

Butterfly: Mourning cloak

Fish: Black-spotted cutthroat trout

Flower: Bitterroot

Tree: Ponderosa pine

Stones: Montana sapphire, Montana agate

Fossil: *Maiasaura* (duck-billed dinosaur)

Ballad: "Montana Melody" with words and music by Carleen and LeGrande Harvey

Western meadowlark

Bitterroot

MONTANA

Joseph Howard, the composer of several hundred popular songs, set Charles Cohan's words to music in 1910. The song was adopted as the official state song in 1945.

Words by Charles C. Cohan

Music by Joseph E. Howard

Highest Point: 12,799 feet above sea level, at Granite Peak

Lowest Point: 1,800 feet above sea level, along the Kootenai River in Lincoln County

Area: 147,047 square miles

Greatest Distance North to South: 321 miles

Greatest Distance East to West: 559 miles

Bordering States: Idaho to the west, Wyoming to the south, North Dakota and South Dakota to the east

Hottest Recorded Temperature: 117 ºF at Glendive on July 20, 1893, and at Medicine Lake on July 5, 1937

Coldest Recorded Temperature: –70 ºF at Rogers Pass on January 20, 1954

Average Annual Precipitation: 15 inches

Major Rivers: Bighorn, Bitterroot, Blackfoot, Clark Fork, Flathead, Gallatin, Jefferson, Kootenai, Madison, Milk, Missouri, Musselshell, Powder, Sun, Yellowstone

Major Lakes: Bighorn, Canyon Ferry, Flathead, Fort Peck, Hebgen, Hungry Horse, Medicine, Tiber

Bighorn sheep

Trees: alder, ash, aspen, birch, cedar, fir, larch, pine, spruce

Wild Plants: aster, blue grama, buffalo grass, columbine, daisy, dryad, lily, lupine, poppy, primrose, western wheatgrass

Animals: bear, beaver, bighorn sheep, bison, deer, elk, mink, moose, mountain goat, muskrat, pronghorn antelope

Birds: bluebird, duck, eagle, goose, grouse, magpie, partridge, pheasant, swan, wren

Fish: crappie, grayling, perch, pike, sauger, sturgeon, trout, walleye, whitefish

Endangered Animals: black-footed ferret, gray wolf, least tern, pallid sturgeon, white sturgeon, whooping crane

Montana History

1700s Assiniboine, Blackfeet, Gros Ventre, Salish (Flathead), Pend d'Oreille, and Kootenai Indians live in what is now Montana.

1740s The first European explorers known to enter the area, François and Louis de la Verendrye, cross the southeastern corner of the present-day state.

1803 Eastern Montana becomes U.S. territory when the United States buys the Louisiana Territory from France.

1805–1806 American explorers Meriwether Lewis and William Clark pass through Montana on their way to the Pacific Ocean and back.

1807 Montana's first fur trading post is built at the confluence of the Bighorn and Yellowstone rivers.

1841 Father Pierre-Jean De Smet, a Catholic priest, founds Saint Mary's Mission, the first permanent European settlement in Montana.

1862 Large deposits of gold are discovered at Grasshopper Creek, near Bannack.

1864 Montana Territory is created.

1876 Sioux, Cheyenne, and Arapaho Indians defeat U.S. troops led by George Armstrong Custer at the Battle of the Little Bighorn.

1880 The Utah and Northern Railway becomes the first railroad to reach Montana.

1881 Copper king Marcus Daly begins mining operations near Butte.

1889 Montana becomes the forty-first state.

1910 Glacier National Park is established.

1916 Jeannette Rankin of Missoula is elected to the U.S. House of Representatives, becoming the first woman to serve in Congress.

1917 A fire on Granite Mountain near Butte kills at least 167 copper miners.

1940 Montana workers complete Fort Peck Dam.

1950s Oil wells begin operating in eastern Montana.

1955 Montana's first aluminum plant begins processing in Columbia Falls.

1967–1968 Butte metal miners hold an eight-month strike, the longest in Montana history.

1969 Open-pit mining for coal begins in southeastern Montana.

1972 Montana voters approve a new state constitution.

1988 Forest fires destroy large stands of Montana timber during a drought.

1994 The U.S. government agrees to protect 1.7 million acres of western Montana land from commercial use.

1999–2006 Montana experiences seven years of drought.

2009 President Barack Obama signs the Recovery and Reinvestment Act, which provides approximately $800 million in federal funding to Montana.

ECONOMY

Agricultural Products: barley, beef cattle, dairy products, hay, mustard, oats, potatoes, safflower, sheep, sugar beets, sunflowers, wheat

Manufactured Products: fertilizer, food products, machinery, refined oil, wood products

Natural Resources: barite, clay, coal, copper, gold, gypsum, lead, limestone, lumber, molybdenum, natural gas, oil, platinum, silver, uranium, zinc

Barley

Business and Trade: health care, real estate, transportation, wholesale and retail trade

Race to the Sky Montana's toughest dogsled drivers brave the cold each February, racing from Lincoln to Holland Lake and back.

National Ski-Joring Finals This March competition in Red Lodge promotes a sport imported from Norway, where horse-drawn skiers swoosh over the snow, past obstacles and over jumps.

Saint Patrick's Day Butte celebrates its Irish roots on March 17 as pipers, drummers, and dancers dressed in green parade through the streets.

Bucking Horse Sale Miles City kicks off the rodeo season in May with this multi-day event, which includes a horse auction, art

National Ski-Joring Finals

Bucking Horse Sale

exhibits, rodeo competitions, and dancing. Watch expert cowboys try to bust each horse—the ones that buck the best are bought for rodeos.

International Wildlife Film Festival Mountain lions and grizzly bears play starring roles at this unusual film festival each spring, when Missoula theaters show the world's best wild animal movies.

Yellowstone River Boat Float For three days in July, boaters follow the route Lewis and Clark took down the Yellowstone River between Livingston and Laurel. Anyone can join the fun using any kind of boat, from a rubber raft to a homemade canoe.

Western Montana Fair

Milk River Indian Days The Gros Ventre and Assiniboine tribes
hold a powwow during the last weekend in July at Fort Belknap.
Dancing, music, and traditional foods are popular at the event.

Sweet Pea Festival Each August Bozeman celebrates the arts with
outdoor concerts, special exhibits, and even dancing lessons.

Crow Fair and Rodeo Indians from all over North America camp
along the Little Bighorn River in August, celebrating their heritage
with dancing, wild horse races, and an all-Indian rodeo.

Western Montana Fair Missoula holds one of the state's biggest
country fairs in August. The fun includes rodeo events, art
displays, a livestock sale, and concerts.

Crow Fair and Rodeo

An Rí Rá Montana Irish Festival The Montana Gaelic Cultural Society holds its annual celebration of all things Irish in August with film screenings, dance workshops and performances, public readings, and concerts.

Nordicfest Many of the families who live in Libby are descended from Norwegian settlers. In September the town gets back to its roots with a weekend of Scandinavian food, music, and dancing.

Montana Chokecherry Festival Lewistown celebrates a tiny, tangy, dark red fruit called the chokecherry, which ripens in Montana each September. A pancake breakfast with chokecherry syrup and a pit-spitting contest are highlights of the event.

STATE STARS

Eric Bergoust (1969–   ) of Missoula is a champion aerial skier. A born daredevil, Bergoust started skiing over his own homemade jumps at age thirteen. In 1998 his quadruple-twisting triple backflips brought him an Olympic gold medal. He also has three U.S. championships and fifteen World Cup victories under his belt.

William A. Clark (1839–1925) was an industrialist whose business empire once spanned Montana. Clark helped shape the state's economy with his banking, transportation, manufacturing, and mining ventures in the nineteenth century. A leader in Democratic politics, he served in the U.S. Senate from 1901 to 1907.

Eric Bergoust

Gary Cooper (1901–1961), born in Helena, was a film star known for his good looks and strong, quiet style. The son of British parents, he spent several years in England attending school. Cooper later returned to Montana and spent some time working on his father's ranch. His handsome cowboy image landed him bit parts in Westerns during the 1920s, and by the 1930s he had become Hollywood's top box office draw. Cooper appeared in more than eighty movies during his lifetime, winning Academy Awards for his performances in *Sergeant York* and *High Noon*. In 1960 he received a special award from the Academy of Motion Picture Arts and Sciences "for his many memorable screen performances and the international recognition he . . . has gained for the motion picture industry."

Marcus Daly (1841–1900), a Montana mining tycoon, moved to the United States from Ireland when he was fifteen. He went west, became an expert miner, and bought a claim to the Anaconda silver mine near Butte. The mine contained a huge vein of copper that made Daly rich in just a few years. Daly also built many Montana banks, power plants, and railroads. In the 1890s he fought William A. Clark for control of state politics in what was known as the war of the copper kings.

Ivan Doig

Ivan Doig (1939–   ) writes vivid stories about Montana and its people. Doig was born in White Sulphur Springs, where his parents were ranch hands. Life in the rural West became the subject of many of his novels. His best-known books include *English Creek* and *This House of Sky*.

A. B. Guthrie Jr. (1901–1991), who grew up in Choteau, wrote novels about the western frontier. Guthrie was one of the first writers to make life in the Old West seem as harsh as it really was. In 1947 he published *The Big Sky*, a realist novel about the days of the mountain men. He won a Pulitzer Prize for his 1949 novel *The Way West*.

Jack Horner (1946–   ) is one of the world's leading dinosaur hunters. Born in Shelby, Horner started digging up fossils when he was in grade school. As an adult, Horner has discovered many amazing fossils, including a nest of baby dinosaurs and several *Tyrannosaurus rex* skeletons. Working at Montana's Museum of the Rockies, he does research on the everyday life of *T. rex* and other dinosaurs of the same size.

Jack Horner

Chet Huntley (1911–1974) was a leading television newscaster. A native of Cardwell, Huntley began his career as a radio announcer in Seattle. He started working in television in 1951. In 1956 Huntley teamed up with David Brinkley on a nightly news program called the *Huntley-Brinkley Report*. The highly rated show won eight Emmy Awards over the next fifteen years. Huntley retired to Montana in the early 1970s.

Dorothy M. Johnson (1905–1984) wrote many gritty, realistic stories about life in the Wild West. Johnson grew up in Whitefish, graduated from the University of Montana, and worked as a magazine editor in New York for many years. Her first works of fiction appeared in the 1940s in the *Saturday Evening Post* and other magazines. Her stories "The Hanging Tree," "A Man Called Horse," and "The Man Who Shot Liberty Valance" were made into popular films.

Evel Knievel (1938–2007), a native of Butte, was a motorcyclist whose death-defying stunts made him a legend. Evel Knievel's career started in 1965 with attention-getting acts such as riding through fire and jumping over mountain lions. Each year his feats got more incredible. In 1974 he tried to jump Idaho's Snake River Canyon in a rocket-powered "sky-cycle." He just missed the edge and parachuted to the canyon floor. By the time he retired in 1975, he had cleared thirteen Mack trucks, sailed over fourteen Greyhound buses, and broken thirty-five bones.

Evel Knievel

Myrna Loy (1905–1993) was a movie actress who charmed millions with her elegant wit and style. Born Myrna Williams in Radersburg, she moved to Helena when she was seven years old. There she made her stage debut at the Harlow Theater with a dance routine at age twelve.

Myrna Loy

After moving with her family to Los Angeles, she began acting in local theater, then in movies. In the 1930s and 1940s her role as Nora Charles in *The Thin Man* made her one of Hollywood's most popular stars. Loy received an honorary Academy Award in 1991.

Norman Maclean (1902–1990) wrote *A River Runs Through It and Other Stories*, a book about a Montana family that became the basis for a successful film. Maclean spent most of his youth in Missoula. He began writing late in life, but his depth and poetic style were immediately admired. A Montana firefighting tragedy is the subject of his last book, *Young Men and Fire*.

Dave McNally (1942–2002) was one of the top baseball pitchers of the 1960s and 1970s. Born in Billings, McNally started playing for the Baltimore Orioles in 1962. Between 1968 and 1971 he gained national fame with four 20-win seasons in a row. McNally was a powerful batter, too. In 1970 he became the only pitcher ever to hit a grand slam in a World Series.

Plenty Coups

Plenty Coups (1848–1932) was a Crow Indian leader born near what is now Billings. When he was a young boy he had a vision that told him white people would invade Crow lands.

Believing the best way to help his people was to keep peace with the whites, he urged the Crow to join forces with the U.S. government in fighting their Indian enemies, the Sioux and Cheyenne. Plenty Coups was named chief of all the Crow in 1904.

Jeannette Rankin (1880–1973) was the first woman to serve in the U.S. Congress. Born near Missoula and educated at Montana State University, Rankin led the fight to get eligible women the right to vote in Montana. In 1916 she was elected to the U.S. House of Representatives, where she supported the state's copper miners and campaigned for the right of all eligible women in the United States to vote. Throughout her life Rankin was also an active advocate for peace, opposing U.S. involvement in World War I, World War II, and Vietnam.

Martha Raye

Martha Raye (1916–1994) was a popular singer and actress. Raye was born in Butte and began appearing onstage with her show-business parents at age three. She later sang, acted in movies, and had her own television variety show. But Raye is best known for her generous spirit in entertaining troops during World War II. Beloved by thousands of U.S. war veterans, Raye won the Jean Hersholt Humanitarian Award from the Academy of Motion Picture Arts and Sciences in 1969 and the Presidential Medal of Freedom in 1993.

Charles M. Russell (1864–1926) was an artist who captured the spirit of the West. Born in Missouri, Russell was sent to Montana at the age of sixteen so he would learn about life the hard way. But Russell loved the West. He found work as a hunter, sheepherder, and cowboy. He began drawing and painting, recording what he saw and re-creating famous western scenes. Russell eventually completed more than four thousand works of cowboy art, and his romantic vision of the West is still strong today.

Harold Urey (1893–1981) was a pioneer in the field of atomic energy. Born in Walkerton, Indiana, Urey earned a bachelor's degree from the University of Montana. He was awarded the Nobel Prize in chemistry in 1934 for discovering deuterium, which was important in the development of nuclear power. During World War II Urey helped create the world's first atomic bomb. Later he became active in the United Nations in the hope that the world would solve its problems more peacefully.

Harold Urey

Peter Voulkos (1924–2002) was an artist whose dramatic clay sculptures can be found in museums around the world. Born in Bozeman, Voulkos began working with clay as a student at Montana State College. He learned to make pots on a potter's wheel and then transformed them by tearing and gashing the surface of the clay. *The Rocking Pot* and *Gallas Rock* are among his best-known works.

James Welch (1940–2003) was a poet and novelist who wrote about modern American-Indian life. Welch's widely acclaimed books include *Winter in the Blood*, *Riding the Earthboy 40*, and *Fools Crow*. He was born in Browning and was a member of the Blackfoot and Gros Ventre tribes.

Lones Wigger (1937–   ) is one of the world's most accurate marksmen. Wigger learned to shoot a rifle on his family's ranch near Great Falls. He joined the U.S. Army Marksmanship Unit and went on to win more than one hundred international shooting awards, including two Olympic gold medals. Wigger is a member of the USA Shooting Hall of Fame.

TOUR THE STATE

Grizzly & Wolf Discovery Center (West Yellowstone) You'll come face to face with Montana's most powerful animals at this wildlife museum. Outdoor exhibits include live bears and wolves.

Grizzly & Wolf Discovery Center

Little Bighorn Battlefield National Monument (Crow Agency)
The Sioux, Cheyenne, and Arapaho Indians wiped out George
Armstrong Custer and his troops on this battlefield in 1876. More
than two hundred men who died in the battle are buried on Last
Stand Hill. The Indian Memorial, dedicated in 2003, was added to
the site to honor the American Indians on both sides who fought
to protect their way of life.

Pictograph Cave State Park (Lockwood) Roughly 4,500 years ago
American Indians began using the Pictograph, Middle, and Ghost
caves located in the park. More than 30,000 artifacts have been
found at the site. Today, visitors can see the paintings that decorate
the walls of the enormous Pictograph Cave.

Pictograph Cave State Park

Little Bighorn Battlefield National Monument

Moss Mansion (Billings) Banking and business king Preston Boyd Moss once owned this lavish home, which was completed in 1903. Much of Moss's elegant furniture is still on display.

Bighorn Canyon National Recreation Area (Fort Smith) Some of Montana's most breathtaking scenery can be found where 1,000-foot-high cliffs tower above Yellowtail Reservoir. Visit Devil Canyon Overlook for the most spectacular view.

Pryor Mountains (South of Billings) Mysterious ice caves are hidden among the limestone peaks on the east side of Bighorn Canyon. Mustangs run free in the mountains' wild horse range.

Bighorn Canyon National Recreation Area

Makoshika State Park

Pompeys Pillar (Billings) Explorer William Clark carved his name
and the date of his visit—July 25, 1806—at the foot of this stone
landmark. He named it Pompey's Tower after the son of his American-
Indian guide, Sacagawea; and it was later renamed Pompeys Pillar.

Makoshika State Park (Glendive) The name of this windblown
sandstone landscape comes from a Sioux word meaning "bad earth"
or "bad land." Check out the colorful rock formations and explore
the park's hiking trails.

Range Riders Museum (Miles City) At this frontier museum you can
visit a one-room schoolhouse, see pioneer weapons and tools along
with American-Indian artifacts, and learn about life at Fort Keogh.

Yellowstone National Park (Cooke City, Gardiner, and West Yellowstone) Only a small strip of this famous preserve is located in Montana, but you can enter the park from three locations in the Big Sky Country. Its natural wonders include bears, beautiful lakes, and spouting geysers.

Saint Mary's Mission (Stevensville) Montana's oldest Catholic mission was established in 1841. You can visit a later version of the mission, which dates back to 1866. The present-day mission stands not far from its original site.

C. M. Russell Museum (Great Falls) Visit the studio of America's favorite cowboy artist in Great Falls. You can check out dozens of his oil paintings, watercolors, and sculptures at the exhibit hall next door.

Flathead Lake (Polson) Summer visitors enjoy boating, fishing, and kayaking in these deep blue waters. Beautiful Wild Horse Island boasts bighorn sheep, wild horses, and seventy-five species of birds.

Aerial Fire Depot and Smokejumper Center (Missoula) This is the place where the bravest workers in the U.S. Forest Service learn to parachute into a blaze. Visitors can tour the parachuting base and learn how smokejumpers stop forest fires.

Glacier National Park (West Glacier) Called the Crown of the Continent, this paradise high in the Rocky Mountains was once the homeland of the Salish, Kootenai, and Blackfeet Indians. Visitors love the Going-to-the-Sun Road, a narrow, winding route that takes them past towering peaks.

First Peoples Buffalo Jump Park (Ulm) Hundreds of years ago Indians drove herds of bison over the cliffs in this park. Today you can walk a trail along the cliffs and enjoy the view.

Grasshopper Glacier (Cooke City) Long ago, swarms of grasshoppers were trapped in the ice at this glacier. They can still be seen today.

Museum of the Rockies (Bozeman) The biggest attraction at this amazing museum are the fossils, including dinosaur eggs and a *Tyrannosaurus rex* skull.

Quake Lake (West Yellowstone) In 1959 a powerful earthquake caused a mountaintop to break off and fall into the Madison River, forming a lake full of huge boulders and drowned trees.

Quake Lake

The world's shortest river, the Roe, connects Giant Springs with the Missouri River near Great Falls. The size of the Roe River shifts with the seasons, but at most it is 200 feet long.

Snowmelt from Triple Divide Peak in Glacier National Park flows toward three different corners of North America. Some of it ends up in the Pacific Ocean. The rest travels east to the Atlantic Ocean or north to Hudson Bay.

The names of Montana towns such as Offer, Opportunity, and Eureka recall the state's mining boom days. But who knows how Big Arm, Square Butte, and Hungry Horse got their names?

Find Out More

If you want to find out more about Montana, check your local library or bookstore for these titles.

GENERAL STATE BOOKS

Stein, R. Conrad. *Montana* (America the Beautiful). New York, NY: Children's Press, 2009.

SPECIAL INTERST BOOKS

Ditchfield, Christin. *The Shoshone*. Danbury, CT: Franklin Watts, 2005.

Levine, Michelle. *The Ojibwe* (Native American Histories). Minneapolis: Lerner Publications, 2007.

Murray, Stuart. *Wild West*. New York: DK Publishing Inc., 2005.

WEBSITES

Montana Field Guide
http://fieldguide.mt.gov/default.aspx
Learn about the plants and animals found in the Treasure State.

Montana for Kids
www.montanakids.com
Find out all kinds of fascinating facts about Montana.

Official Montana Site

www.mt.gov

Learn more about the state's government, economy, and history at its official site.

Index

Page numbers in **boldface** are illustrations and charts.

Clayton Bennett is a writer who has visited Montana many times over the past twenty-five years. He has fished for trout in the Boulder River, photographed lightning in Paradise Valley, and hiked up Emigrant Peak. He has toured the state by both train and car and is looking forward to another visit soon. Bennett lives in Minnesota, which has no mountains.

Wendy Mead is a freelance writer and editor. In her work she has tackled a variety of subjects for young readers, ranging from birds to biographies. She has coauthored two other titles, *Arizona* and *Utah*, in the Celebrate the States series.

WITHDRAWN